The
PLEASURE OF GARDENING

CONSERVATORY GARDENING

A complete practical guide

LYNN BRYAN

ANAYA
PUBLISHERS LTD

CONTENTS

Introduction

Since I decided to write this book, memories of conservatories I have known have filled my mind. The first was one of the more interesting. Attached to a large and rambling Victorian house, it was built in the traditional shape with small pane-glass windows as walls, and glass panels soaring to a wrought-iron framed roof. The family who owned this space were Russian émigrés full of lively character and the conservatory reflected their exuberant lifestyle. Tame birds lived among its green foliage, bicycles were always leant against the dark green wrought-iron and timber seat (perfect for three); the wrought-iron table with its elegant curled legs was the hub of social activity. Children learned about plant cultivation in here, sneaked their first kiss in the palms, and entertained friends and family with hide-and-seek and charades.

A well-read copy of Pravda seemed at home lying on the benchtop next to primula and various seedlings. I remember this haven fondly, and not at all romantically. I can still picture the rust, the dusty windowpanes, and the soil that spilled everywhere (this family was not meticulous). Every detail adds pleasure to the memory.

Another conservatory belonged to a friend with whom I had temporarily lost touch. We were living in an unfamiliar part of London, and every day my small son and I walked past a splendid house built on the corner of our street. We would peer through the (clean) windowpanes at the magic world inside seeming to us to overflow with lush growth. Imagine my surprise when a mutual friend gave me the address of the friend for whom I was searching—she lived in the house on the street corner! I spent many idyllic days visiting this elegant conservatory, admiring the floral-covered armchairs and the wicker tables, and that was when I realized the importance of a room like a conservatory. Not only does it act as a transition from the house to the garden, but has an important social role to play in our lives.

Building a conservatory onto your house does not necessarily mean you have to have a passion to fill it with rare and exotic species, although those with flowers and ferns are always the most successful spaces. If the decision to build a conservatory is the result of a need for extra living space (perhaps an adults-only area), then the relaxed atmosphere it creates will add another dimension to the mood of the house.

A great deal of pleasure is to be found among living plants. The conservatory comes into its own during the winter and early spring when it may be too cold to go for long into the garden, and in inclement weather, such a light-filled space provides a buffer between the elements and the warmth of your home. The variety of shapes and fragrances to be found in indoor plants allows you to reflect your personality, and the flooring, the furniture, and the types of containers used combine to make your style statement. What better way is there to make a personal statement! As a resting place, somewhere for the mind to ponder while the hands come into contact with the earth, the conservatory is a priority.

OPPOSITE: This long and narrow conservatory incorporates a few of the important design elements of a truly traditional style room: a tessellated tile floor, free-standing wrought-iron plant stands, scrolled iron work around the window frames, an ancient wicker chair, and sections of trellis on the wall to encourage climbers. Anyone for breakfast?

A POTTED HISTORY

In the traditional vernacular, a conservatory is a place attached to, or inside, the house where plants can be conserved and sheltered from the weather. The idea of bringing plants indoors at night, or in colder weather, reaches back at least as far as the 1st century AD when the Romans learned that if they put trays of fruits and vegetables into nearby caves on cool nights, the plants grew more successfully. Many centuries later, in 1543, a unique garden was created in Pisa, Italy, to allow study of the best ways to protect plants. Early structures built for the purpose were made of wood or stone and featured shutters designed to regulate air and light. In 17th century Holland, simple structures known as orangeries were built to nurture citrus trees and other varieties of fruits. The concept was adopted and further developed in other European countries and these orangeries become a familiar addition to grander homes. Enclosed structures made of wood, stone, or brick, the orangeries sometimes featured panes of glass along the wall which faced the sun. Early methods of heating these enclosures included cast-iron furnaces and the wonderful European tiled stoves. Heat control, unless tended to regularly, was often less than perfect.

By the late 17th century, the delicate citrus fruits growing in these early greenhouses were joined by other varieties of plants. Further development of the conservatory arose from the interest of the upper and middle classes in Europe in the procuring and displaying of rare

exotic plants, brought back by botanists and explorers of the New World and the Pacific Ocean.

Naturally, the act of showing one's newest acquisitions gave rise to a new form of social entertainment, and the conservatory came to be seen as an extra room of the house. Architects and designers were challenged to create walls and windows for these new structures that could be added onto houses. The Industrial Revolution in 19th century England coincided with this desire to show off exotic, tropical plants and thus the conservatory turned into a splendid room, with panes of newly created glass set in strips of timber. A new status symbol was created as the cost of these wonderful fantasies came within the reach of the expanding middle classes. Technology gave architects a new material to use—cast iron. This enabled curves, arches, vaults, and domes to be included in conservatory design. Elegance was the key word in construction.

The epitome of style in the Victorian era was the magnificent Palm House at Kew Gardens—its shape has been admired and copied in miniature versions ever since it opened in the late 1830s. Palms like those within its glass walls were sought after, as were other temperate plants such as ferns, tropical fruit trees, and tropical waterlilies, bright passionflowers, bougainvillea, scented jasmines and other climbers and vines, clerodendrons, and myriad orchid species.

Within the design restrictions of these Victorian conservatories, the plants

were placed in tubs and pots in beds running along either side and in the middle of the space. Tiled or paved paths led one rigidly through masses of plants, grouped mainly according to botanical species. Many public conservatories still follow this design.

Some private collectors specialized, growing numerous varieties of cool ferns or grape vines or rare and exotic species set amidst pools, fountains, and waterfalls.

Heating these interiors was a challenge met by ingenious minds. The British and the Dutch had earlier experimented with underfloor heating. Stoves were built under the floor of the conservatory, burning bark and dry manure to produce heat. Later developments meant that larger boilers could be placed on the exterior of the building, piping hot water through the glasshouse at an even temperature. Designers were careful to prevent too much or too little heat reaching the interior as both of these conditions are injurious to fragile plants.

In the Edwardian era, when heating costs were lowered, the conservatory became as much a leisure room as an indoor garden.

After the turn of the 20th century, the popularity of the conservatory began to decline. Reasons given for this decline vary, but it seems likely that, together with a movement toward a more natural style of garden design promoted by well-known gardener of the time, Gertrude Jekyll, there was a desire to see less elitism in society. The conservatory was a visible symbol of such privilege, and changing social patterns and attitudes lessened its appeal, as did the fact that women became more a part of the workforce after the First World War. Gone for these upper and middle-class women was the pleasure of gardening.

This book is the result of my interest in the phenomenon of the conservatory, and a direct response to the worldwide resurrection of interest in gardening and entertaining in the conservatory. In the following pages, you will find commonsense advice on what type of conservatory is best for your house and how to maintain it. There is advice on which plants to choose for year-round pleasure in this indoor garden and on how to control pests and diseases which, unfortunately, attack even the best-tended plants.

You will also be inspired. A conservatory is a special place, one where keen gardeners can pursue their passion even in the midst of the fiercest winter. The planting illustrations have been designed to encourage you to be imaginative with conservatory schemes. Use this book as a guide to creating your ideal conservatory and planting it in a way that will give you and your family a great deal of pleasure for many years.

RIGHT: Classical stone columns soar into arches in this magnificent stone structure at Flintham in Nottinghamshire, England. Planting is in shady areas, yet note that the amount of light provided by the design is more than adequate.

THE CONSERVATORY

A Room to View

For the purposes of this book, a conservatory is defined as a place with glass walls where a wide variety of plants are grown throughout the year, and as a room for entertaining friends and family. Although this is a beginner's guide, providing information for readers contemplating making a substantial investment in their property, even experienced hothouse gardeners will find inspiration as to how to create a sensational conservatory using the precious plants they have grown in the hothouse.

LEFT: This new addition suits the form of the older home to which it has been attached. Located to the rear in the established garden, it is well sited to catch the sun. The brick base reflects the brick pattern framing the windows in the house; the white drapes soften the look. The glass roof is gently peaked, with a row of ironwork as a final decoration.

PREVIOUS PAGE: This conservatory, designed in the traditional manner, has been successfully added onto this established brick house. The design allows full sun for most of the day, with doors leading onto a paved patio with steps leading down to the main garden. It sits well in relation to the lawn, and fits well with the style of the house.

There are two kinds of conservatories—the cool and the warm. The former is ideal for nearly all of the plants that grow in temperate zones (from 40°F to 55°F, or 4°C to 13°C). The warm conservatory is one that is (obviously) heated for human comfort, is ideal for plants that thrive in a dry, centrally heated environment (especially in winter), and one that is sunlit in summer. More detailed information about these different types of conservatories and plants is in Chapter Three and Chapter Five.

A constant temperature is the key to successful gardening in this miniature ecosystem. The control of sunlight and air humidity is made easier these days by modern technology in the form of automatic electric humidifiers and automatic temperature control systems.

Yet the success of a conservatory is determined by other considerations. First, there is the matter of budget. The more money, the more "extras" you can afford to modify the environment. If you have a modest budget, do not despair. There are early decisions that will be of benefit to all conservatory owners. Read a variety of books, magazines, and conservatory brochures to consolidate in your mind the features that you want for your investment.

WHERE TO SITE?

Ideally, the conservatory ought to be physically attached to the house, since part of its role is to act as a link between the house and the garden. Consider whether to place the structure at the front or the back or even at the side of the house if there is enough space between house and the boundary.

If you do not have a large garden, investigate the possibility of siting your conservatory on top of a flat-roofed extension, or on the roof itself. The same siting considerations apply.

It is also a good idea to build the conservatory away from where howling gales regularly hit the house. This will save heating costs. Plants do not like bad drafts.

Take time to consider where to site the conservatory. Most importantly, check the local building authority codes prior to planning. In which direction is your house oriented? Does it face north, south, east or west? Observe where the sun shines from—does it rise in the front of your home, move around the side, and set at the back? Or vice versa? The answer to this will affect the amount of heat and light the plants will receive.

ORIENTATION

South facing

In the northern hemisphere, this position captures the hottest sun for the longest period. This is not necessarily the best situation, as heat builds quickly, yet it is ideal as a haven for cacti and other plants that like a hot, dry atmosphere. Shading and good ventilation are essential in this position.

In the southern hemisphere, this position creates cooler conditions and it is necessary to consider installing a heating system during winter.

North facing

In the northern hemisphere, heat and light levels are lowest in this situation. Plants that like cooler conditions will thrive here. Ferns and ivies in particular do not like to be hot.

In the southern hemisphere, this position captures the hottest sun for the longest period of the day so it is best to avoid building a conservatory in this position in areas with hot summers.

East and west facing

Ideally situated for most plant and human habitation. A conservatory in this position will see a good measure of sunlight in the morning and afternoon through to evening. In areas where the summers are hot, west-facing structures are to be avoided.

SIZE

Generally speaking, most conservatories are built with a dual purpose in mind—as a haven for plants and as an extra living room. At the planning stage, consider building the largest that you can afford. It is short-sighted to be restrictive. However, a conservatory half the size of your present home will look ridiculous so also consider its proportion to both the house and the garden. Conservatory companies are experts at this and it is advisable to consult a reputable company at an early stage. Architects and landscape designers also can provide an advisory service at this early stage should you want to build the conservatory yourself but need help with the design and planning.

It is wise to work on the ratio of 1 square foot of glazing to 4 square feet (or 1sq m to 4sq m) of floor area. This will help you to maintain a room temperature of 66°F to 70°F (19°C to 21°C).

ABOVE: This contemporary conservatory incorporates traditional elements—the peaked glass roof, arched timber windows set with small panes of glass, and a hard-wearing tiled floor. The addition of pots outside tie the house (located quite close, just out of frame to the left to the conservatory) to the new structure. It is used as an informal living space as well as for growing plants.

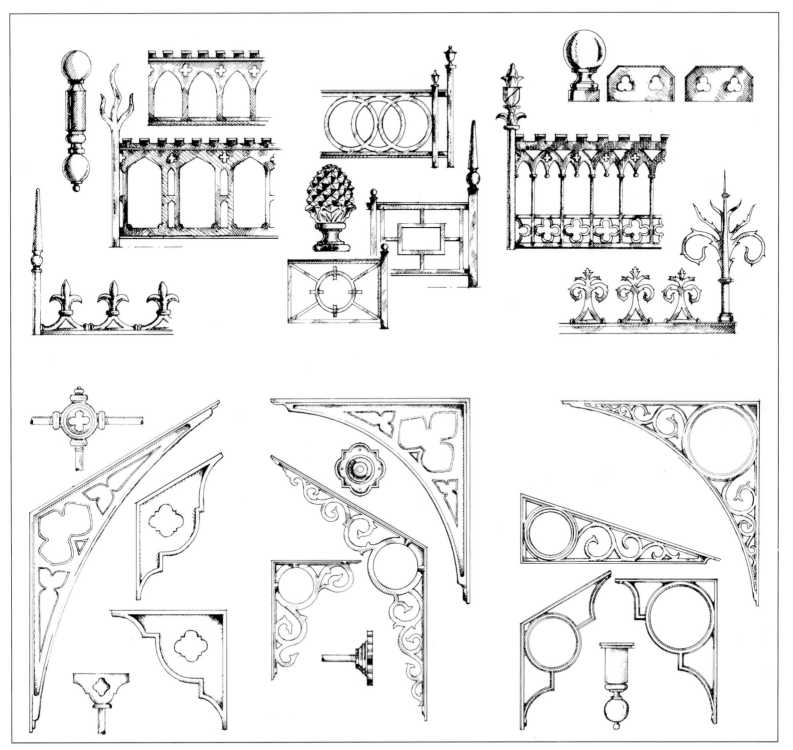

TOP: *A collection of popular, traditional designs for finials, crestings and galleries.*
ABOVE: *A range of designs for traditional support castings.*

STYLE

Ideally, a conservatory should be in a style similar to that of your house. A contemporary structure added to an historic or period-style house will look as if it is an afterthought, whereas one in the same architectural style will, in time, look as if it has been there since the house was built. Decorative features—scrolled ironwork, window arches, crown railings, timber finials—should match too.

Familiarity with the graceful lines and proportions of traditional conservatories leads many people to emulate this appealing romantic style. White-painted timber frames, clear glass inset with Gothic timber cut-out arches, a wrought-iron crown railing on a saddle-back roof, cast-iron columns, a peaked glass roof—these are the decorative embellishments many conservatory owners are intrigued by and desire to re-create. A variety of reproduction styles are available through conservatory companies.

Technological advances have enabled such companies to offer simple, flexible designs that can be sold as complete prefabricated units or in component form. This allows you to design and install a structure of the right shape and size to suit your property—at a price to suit your budget.

As well, many companies offer a custom-design service to match the architectural style of an existing house, down to the tiniest detail, and complete with underfloor heating, shades, automatic temperature, and watering systems—even plants.

Read the fine print on the sales contract to check exactly what services they are providing for the cost. Some questions to ask are:

• Is the company aware of your local area's building regulations?

• Will the company arrange for the preparation of the building site (digging foundations and proper drainage, etc) and manage construction?

• Is all plumbing and electrical wiring included in the quote?

• Are window and door fittings included?

• Are decorative details such as ornamental moldings or brass fittings considered an extra?

• Does the quote include single or double glazing?

Doubleglazing is an excellent energy-saving "extra" and worth considering, especially if you intend to use the conservatory at night. The heat from the day's sunshine will linger longer.

Investigate the use of special paint-based coatings on panes of glass for further insulation.

LEFT: This conservatory catches the sun; and as a protection against the heat, white fabric is draped from the height of the main wall to the exterior window frames. A ceiling fan also controls the temperature. Planting has been kept to the inside wall, and to the end of the room, away from direct sunlight. A lion's head sits in the midst of a passionflower vine climbing up the wall.

THE FLOOR PLAN

When considering the layout, think about how you will use the space. Most conservatories will be added to an existing room and entered from that room via a door or double doors situated either in a central position or at one end. There may also be an external door. The obvious location for a dining table and chairs or a large seating arrangement of sofa and chairs is in the middle of the space. The most important consideration is to be able to place furniture away from foot-traffic paths and busy gardening areas. Bumping into and leaning over chairs while pruning or reaching for the potting mixture will become annoying.

Built-in, waist-height workbenches are ideal for indoor gardening. Underneath, on shelves, you can store pots and containers, fertilizers, slug pellets, and watering cans.

Freestanding wrought-iron or timber plant stands are attractive features to add to the conservatory. See Chapter Four for details and inspiration on decorative features and fixtures.

OTHER DETAILS TO CONSIDER

• Do you need a power outlet on the workbench top for a small music stereo unit?

• Are you going to serve coffee and tea in the conservatory? You may need a power outlet for the kettle or the coffee machine.

• For dinner parties, you will need a power outlet for the heated hostess

trolley (if you use one). They are terrific if the kitchen is located some distance from the conservatory.

• Do you want a freestanding light next to a chair or sofa to read by? The power outlet for this can be set into a water-tight unit on the floor if it is planned in advance. Then there is no problem with wires snaking across the floor.

FLOORING

For true indoor gardeners, the floor sur-face must be practical. Stone paving slabs, concrete slabs, terracotta tiles (large or small), square hard-wearing ceramic tiles, and bricks are ideal, and each surface has its unique appeal. Marble tiles create a sophisticated, ele-gant look for rooms which will be used more for entertaining than for serious gardening.

Consider how water is to be drained away—perhaps have a discreet drainhole under the shelving units, near the faucet or tap, and another near the larger plants. You may prefer one long narrow drain, covered with a decorative grille, to run along one side of the conservatory.

DECORATIVE LIGHTING

At night, a conservatory is a very roman-tic place. Several elements make it thus: the fragrance of the flowers, the architec-tural style, and mood lighting.

With the variety of shapes, styles, and low-wattage lights now available, it needs only a good lighting plan to make the conservatory one of the most interesting night rooms in your home. If you design the lighting plan yourself,

ABOVE: Grey, white and pale aqua blue tiles in a traditional design surround a patterned heating vent set into the floor. This type of heating vent is one of the best solutions to temperature control, especially if the air conditioning system is thermostatically controlled.

OPPOSITE PAGE: A sophisticated elegance is achieved with the marble tiled floor, wrought-iron furniture and a central circular light fitting. The chintz curtaining fabric has a floral theme to set the mood at the entrance doors. Plants are contained in pots placed symmetrically to either side of the doors at the far end.

do so at the planning stage, not after the structure is finished. Use a piece of graph paper to draw a scale drawing of the conservatory space. Work out where you want the wall or ceiling fit-tings and power outlets to go, and mark them on your plan. This can be trans-ferred to the electrician's copy of the builder's plan.

Style is an important consideration, but practicality is important, too. For example, hanging lights sometimes hang in the most inconvenient places because of structural restrictions, and people end up bumping their heads on the lightshades. Try to incorporate subtle spotlighting to accent ferns and elegant, tall palms. Use discreetly hidden lights in plants grouped on the floor or on lower levels. Both conventional lights and modern low-voltage halogen lights (these have their own transformers) create a brilliant effect with dark shadows thrown onto a wall. Do be careful not to place a light so that it touches the leaves, as too much heat is detrimental to the plant.

Any lighting installation should be done by a registered electrician. For safety, all electrical connections must be waterproof and the whole system fitted with a trip switch or circuit breaker in case of watery accidents.

HEATING THE CONSERVATORY

This is a great challenge. Maintaining a correct and even temperature in a conservatory presents many aspects to consider. If you intend to use the space for leisurely living as well as for growing subtropical plants, a compromise is essential. The plant must be happy in its environment and so must you. You will have an immediate advantage if your conservatory is attached to the side of the house. Heat from the house may warm the area through the common wall—usually brick—which retains heat well.

How hot your conservatory will be depends on how much sun streams into it at the hottest time of the day. If you live in a region where the winters are harsh and the outside temperature regularly falls below freezing, you must plan the heating carefully and consider double glazing all or part of the

ABOVE: This heating grid is set into stone paving slabs and attracts the variegated foliage of the Wandering Jew plant, Zebrina pendula, *and the magnificent* Dracaena *species (left), leafy members of the Lily family.*

conservatory. There are steps to take just prior to a chilly winter. Make a thorough visual check of the windows, particularly slatted windows, to see that they are closing properly. On the doors, replace old weather-strip sealant to prevent heat loss.

Temperatures of 60°F to 70°F (15°C to 21°C) are fine for both plants and humans. Try to keep an even temperature through each season. Plant experts recommend that you do not let the temperature drop below 45°F (7°C) in winter. With the tremendous range of quality heating systems now available in most countries, temperature control is a matter of balance between necessity and your budget.

Some heating options are:

• Electric convection heaters — considered to be cheaper than gas heaters and they cause less condensation.

• A ducted system leading from a central boiler — either solid fuel or a wet system using wood.

• An extension of a central heating unit — warm air circulating through air-conditioning grilles set either in the floor or in the walls.

• A solar heating unit.

• Underfloor heating (expensive but very good) — suitable only for concrete floors. This can be run at off-peak hours to maintain a steady warmth, and is best used as a background heat.

• Hot water-filled radiators placed at regular intervals throughout the space. An electric timing unit is excellent for controlling temperature and, of course, the amount of power or energy consumed. It makes it easier to budget monthly bills.

Whichever heating system you choose, you will need to have a thermostat separate from the central domestic system so that it can operate night and day in cold winter months.

VENTILATION

To cool a conservatory in the height of summer, a good ventilation system is essential. Open doors leading into the house and leading into the garden create a through draft (or cross-ventilation) — an environment similar to that of a natural breeze, which plants are used to.

Open windows create the same effect. (If you choose to place slatted windows in the wall, check they are waterproof as some types leak and let in unnecessary cold air on chilly winter nights.) Opening windows set into the roof are a benefit as they act as an exhaust, allowing the rising hot air to escape. A variety of styles are on the market, with a choice of timber, steel, or metal frames. A central ceiling fan is also a consideration for good circulation of air.

WATERING SYSTEMS

A basic requirement in a conservatory is a faucet or tap placed in a convenient location. You may like just to use an old-fashioned watering can, or you may choose to install a sophisticated automatic watering system. The new systems are wonderful, with devices that indicate when a certain plant needs watering, but they are expensive. Check with the garden expert at the plant store as to which will be suitable for your needs.

As a rule, plants need more water in summer — check the soil every day.

Be careful not to overwater. If you do, the soil will look water-logged, the plant's leaves will appear unhealthy and droopy; the way you feel on a hot and humid day. Check the quality of your soil or compost — peat-based composts require more watering than soil composts. Take note of the difference in the speed with which water is absorbed by the different soil types. Judge how much water individual plants need by experimenting daily.

The type of pot or container affects water requirements, too. Plastic pots retain water; unglazed pots let moisture evaporate. Pots and containers with matching bases are adequate, as are old saucers. The latter add a decorative touch, too. Take extra care with hanging plants as water tends to evaporate more quickly in this situation.

There are moisture-measuring instruments on the market, but your eye is the best judge. When watering, ensure you aim the stream at the roots, not all over the plant. A gentle spray is adequate for flowers and buds — use an empty household plastic spray bottle, washed thoroughly. It will work well to give a misty spray for special plants.

If the plant's container has a base, pour a reasonable quantity of water into the base. The roots will grow down toward the water.

Self-watering pots, with level indicators, are a good idea if you are often away from home for extended periods. Refill these pots according to the manufacturer's instructions.

USEFUL TIPS

• Check the acidity of your water supply and if necessary attach a water filter to lessen the lime, fluoride, and chlorine content.

• The ideal time of the day to water is early morning, or early evening, when the heat of the day has dissipated. This can be a leisurely activity, one for taking time out of a busy schedule and contemplating the pleasure of gardening on a small scale.

PLANTING THE SEED

Propagation

Walking into a plant nursery to behold rows and rows of tiny plants stretched out along the shelves is a gardener's delight. For these tiny plants represent a future full of glorious blooms and foliage. The miracle of the natural growth cycle is about to gradually unfold with the seasons. It is possible to begin that cycle yourself in your conservatory with cuttings from existing plants. For beginners, the more common and easy-to-raise plants are ideal.

PLANTS FROM SEEDS

Sowing seed is considered a difficult way to propagate a plant. The act of sowing is simple; the difficulty is in maintaining the correct warmth and humidity for plant growth. Still, there is much personal satisfaction to be had when you see the first signs of a new plant poking through the soil.

Here is how to sow seeds. Fill a wooden or cardboard box or small plant pot almost to the top with a soil mixture or compost mixture especially for seeds (the mixture is known by different names but is essentially the same product). Carefully, let the seeds drop from between your fingertips into the soil. Cover the seeds with a fine layer of the soil or compost mix. Seeds need air so do not smother them. Place in a little water in a bucket or bowl to allow the soil to soak up the water. Take the pot out when the top of the soil feels damp to your touch. Drain for a couple of hours. Then cover the seed container with a sheet of glass or a piece of clear plastic and place in a warm cupboard. Check the glass or plastic for condensation and wipe clear each day.

Ensure a supply of air to the container once or twice a day for good ventilation.

When the seedlings poke through the surface of the soil, move the container into the light. Avoid direct sunlight as the seedlings are still fragile and may burn.

As the seedlings grow, thin them, carefully snipping out the weak plants at soil level.

Use your judgment as to when to pot the seedlings into small individual pots. Generally, the best time is when they look big enough to handle easily. Soon each young plant will need potting-on, using a potting compost to encourage further growth. It is important at this stage to avoid sudden changes in light, humidity, or temperature.

Many keen indoor gardeners prefer to use a heated propagator to increase the range of plants that can be grown from seed.

TIP

Save work by planting seeds in commercially available strips of compressed soil or compost instead of in loose material.

PLANTS FROM STONES

Avocado

You must have tried to grow a plant from a stone or a pip at some stage. (Children frequently try it as a school project!) Place an avocado stone in water, supported by two matchsticks resting on the edge of a round wine glass. Place on a window ledge. After eight to 10 weeks, strong white roots will burst through the skin. When you spy a single shoot, transfer the seedling to a pot filled with compost mixture. Et voilà! You have an avocado plant.

OPPOSITE: A marvellous display of height and balance in this grouping of pelargoniums, fuchsias and the richly coloured coleus in the conservatory at Falkland Palace in England.

PREVIOUS PAGE: For sheer elegance, one cannot go past this small deciduous orchid (Pleione sp.) from Asia, seen here in all of its beauty.

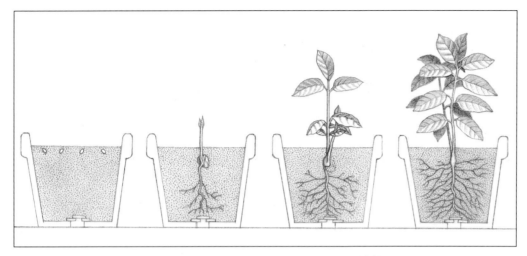

CREATING PLANTS FROM PIPS AND STONES
Citrus fruit are easy to germinate from seeds. Place a few seeds into small pots filled with
quality potting mixture. Keep in a warm environment. Seedlings will appear after two to three
weeks. Pull out the weaker ones, leaving the stronger to grow with space.

Pips

To get pips to grow happily, place several large pips from an orange, lemon, or grapefruit into small pots containing potting compost. Maintain a temperature of around 60°F (16°C). Within weeks, seedlings will appear. Thin out the weaklings and encourage the rest as you would a young plant.

PLANTS FROM LEAF CUTTINGS

It is a miracle that you can grow plants just from leaf cuttings. The easiest plants with which to do this are African violets (*Saintpaulia ionantha*) and begonias (*Begonia rex*).

Water is all that is needed for *Saintpaulia* leaf cuttings to take root. Fill two-thirds of a shallow jar with water. Cover the jar with metal foil punched with small holes. Cut healthy-looking leaves from the plant and place their stems through the holes in the foil, making sure the ends reach the water. It takes four to five weeks for roots to emerge, followed soon after by small plant forms. When these are big enough to handle, cut from the old leaf and place in a small pot filled with potting mixture and watch the growth.

You can also propagate leaves from these plants in potting mixture. Pot the potting mixture in the bottom of a shallow container, adding a thin layer of sand. Gently pick a leaf from a healthy plant and quickly dip the end into a saucer of rooting hormone powder. Make a few holes in the sand with an old pen or pencil and push the cutting into the hole. Water. Insert a wire frame over the leaf, cover this with a plastic bag to extend down over the plant and the rim of the pot. This will create a humid environment for the leaf to grow. Small plants will appear at the base of the leaf in about two weeks. When they seem big enough to handle, cut the new growth away from the leaf and pot.

PLANTS FROM STEM CUTTINGS

When you buy small young plants from the nursery, they have probably been raised from cuttings, ready to sell. Trying to create more plants from what you have in your own conservatory is a good idea, but while some plants are happy reproducing themselves from stem cuttings, others are not.

Hormone rooting powder is essential to aid the growing process, as is good-quality compost mixture. Cut a 5inch (12cm) length of healthy stem sprouting young leaves and trim the leaves from the lower part.

Place in a small pot filled nearly to the rim with a moist potting and sand mixture. Make a hole with an old pen or pencil, and poke the stem in, firming the mixture as you do so. Keep out of direct sunlight until hardy. Spray daily with a fine mist.

If you are attempting to propagate several stems at a time, it is best to use a shallow plastic tray or container with drainage holes punched in the bottom. Plant in the same way.

If you are serious about mass propagation, purchase of an electric propagator complete with thermostat control. Ask the expert at your local nursery or make enquiries at a local gardening club as to which brand is most reliable and suitable for your purpose.

PROPAGATING STEM CUTTINGS

Choose a growing tip about 4in (10cm) long and cut cleanly immediately below a joint in the stem. Strip off the leaves from the lower part of the stem. Place stem in hormone rooting powder, then into compost and wait for about 10 days for roots to appear. You can try this in water but in compost is a better method.

ABOVE: This is a working conservatory with rows of plants in pots on the work bench and in an area on the ground reserved for re-potting activity. Note the fabulous hanging fuchsia and the rampant clematis.

GETTING THE RIGHT MIXTURE

The soil or compost mixture you use is crucial for successful conservatory gardening. Do not use soil from your garden beds in pots. Use a commercial or home-made potting mixture containing a balanced blend of elements. Commercially packed mixtures are sterilized to kill pests and diseases and their consistency allows easy drainage, yet retains moisture. Some mixtures have been formulated to suit particular plant types.

These mixtures are either soil-based or peat-based. The soil-based type tend to be more expensive as they contain loam, but they store plant nutrients and hold moisture well. Peat-based, soil-less composts are less expensive (they do not contain loam) and are made up of equal parts of peat and washed sand or grit to make a general purpose mixture. The addition of sand or grit improves drainage. When making up a peat potting mixture ensure it is moist, with dry sand mixed in.

It is not just lime-loathing plants that require special consideration when it comes to soil mixtures. Special mixtures for potting cacti and orchids are available from garden nurseries and specialist suppliers.

POTTING ON

There is a wonderful term used by gardeners to describe the process of removing a plant from one pot and placing in another, larger container. This is "potting on".

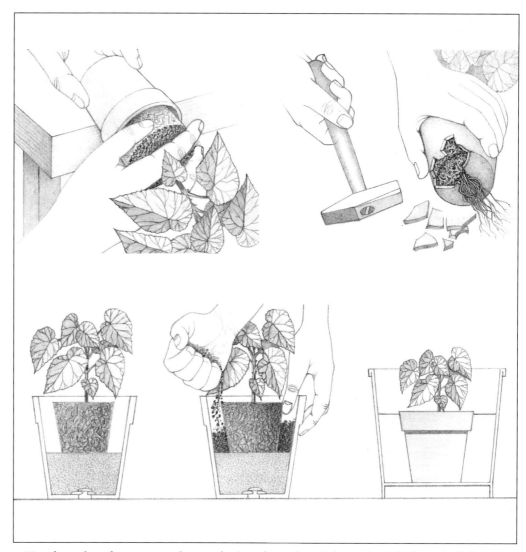

To take a plant from its pot, place one had on the surface of the potting mix, beneath the leaves, and turn pot upside down. Tap the rim gently against the work bench — the ball of soil should come away easily. Check if the roots are peeking through the drainage hole at the bottom of the pot — if they are, then break the pot as pulling roots through the hole will damage the plant. Prior to re-potting place a layer of small, broken pottery chips in the bottom of the new pot. Gently place the plant into the middle of the pot, then ease the mixture into the space around it, pressing down firmly. Soak the re-potted plant in a bucket or bowl of water thoroughly. Then place back in its favourite position.

Plants do become pot-bound; their roots wrap around each other in an unhealthy tangle and finally strangle their own growth. Desperate roots dangle out of the bottom of the pot, seeking relief and food. As previously noted, young plants also need potting on. It is advisable to water plants four to five days before potting on. Potting on is slightly different from re-potting. It means you completely remove the old potting soil from around the roots, then re-pot. When re-potting, you do not necessarily remove all of the soil from around the plant's roots as this can often send the plant into a mild state of shock.

Put aside an hour or two to carry out a thorough and systematic check of all your plants in smaller pots or containers. (The larger plants in heavy pots need more of a combined strength. You will need asistance.) The best time to "pot on" is in spring when the roots are active and able to grow into the new compost mixture, which must be the same type as that in which the plant has been successfully growing.

Place your whole hand over the top of the soil in the pot, with your fingers going around the plant's stem. Gently ease the plant out of the pot and look closely to see if the roots are wrapped thickly around the compost mixture. (Here is an interesting observation: the roots of a plant grown in a clay pot follow the path of the water which has passed through the compost to the sides of the pot. In plastic pots, the roots travel down and then spread out.)

Are there any bugs living in the root matter? If so, pick them off and kill them quickly. Spread newspaper on your work area so that it is easier to clean up afterward. Line up all the plants that must be dealt with as it saves time to do them all at once.

Have the new pot or container handy, the bottom lined with small pebbles or gravel. This encourages good drainage. About an inch and a half (5cm) more soil space is enough to encourage growth. (Friends of mine once put a quite modest-sized plant into a much larger container; the poor thing looked absolutely lost and it wilted away.) If possible, replant in a similar type of container as before because growing conditions are different between plastic and clay pots. Add fresh potting mixture and ease the plant into the new pot or container, patting it firmly and carefully into its new position.

Plants grow at different rates and some, like the larger perennials, may require repotting two or three times a year. Simply remove the plant from its pot as described previously, and trim the root ball, removing any damaged roots.

Lay the large pot on its side and loosen the soil from the edge of the pot, and pull gently, easing the plant from the pot. In severe cases, you may have to break the pot to release the plant. A plant's needs are different, depending on whether it is in a growth or dormant phase. It is best to repot mature plants just prior to a growth season.

As the larger plants grow older, they may need repotting but not "potting on". In that case, carefully tease loose some of the old compost from the roots and replace with new soil mixture. In some circumstances, try removing the top half an inch (2cm) of soil from the pot and replace it with fresh soil.

HANGING AND WALL-MOUNTED BASKETS

Prepare baskets before adding soil and plants by adding a lining of sphagnum moss, available from your local nursery or craft store. The moss has a wonderful texture and the same piece can be used again when you transfer the plant to its new container, as long as you feel the moss is still thick enough to carry on its task of protection and absorption.

Practical but less attractive is plastic sheeting (generally black). Spongy liners, which are also commercially available, will not last as long as the moss. When planting or repotting hanging plants, make small holes for water drainage in the bottom of the lining, or the roots will become waterlogged. Fill the lined container with potting mixture. Trailing plants need exit holes, so make slits in the side of the lining big enough for you to gently push the root ball into. Add more potting mixture to cover the roots.

Before placing the basket into position, it is a good idea to completely immerse it in a tub of water, then drain before hanging.

Treat wall-mounted baskets in the same way.

PRUNING AND TRAINING

Pruning is an important part of the plant's life cycle, particularly in an indoor situation. Pruning encourages growth. When the top shoot is snipped, even more growth replaces it. You end up with a bushier plant instead of one that is straggly and lanky.

Pruning above soil is necessary to keep the plant beautiful. Done on a regular basis, you can lead the plant gently in the direction you wish it to grow. If you leave it until after the plant has happily gone off in its own direction, corrective pruning may not be successful. If climbing plants or vines look as if they are going to take over, use secateurs to control their growth .

Succulents, ferns, and rare species just need tender care—remove dead, dying, or diseased leaves.

Stopping is a mild form of pruning and entails pinching out the growing part of a plant to encourage it to produce new shoots. Ivy responds well to this treatment, as does *Tradescantia* which becomes straggly unless stopped regularly.

Hardwood pruning involves cutting into the old part of the stems. It is a drastic measure to take and is to be avoided if possible. Yet if you inherit a neglected plant and want it to survive, hardwood pruning is unavoidable. This action encourages the dormant eye buds under the bark of the stem to put out new growth. As this is brutal, it is advisable to prune only two or three stems at a time, not the whole plant. Begonias and oleanders (*Nerium oleander*) require harsh pruning or they grow straggly.

Softwood pruning involves cutting away new growth, resulting in two or more shoots growing where previously one grew. This process is good for encouraging more flowers on

hydrangeas and fuchsias. Cut these plants back at the end of the flowering season to encourage new shoots. The most important piece of advice is to watch your plants closely and see what happens after you prune. Make a note of the time of year, and keep a diary of consequences.

Root pruning encourages an outbreak of new root hairs, through which the plant takes its nutrients. Prune the roots in a growth phase. All you need is a decent-sized sharp knife. Having remembered to water the plant three or four days beforehand, gently take it out of its pot. Place the root ball on your work table and slice away at the roots and compost (see illustration). Do not be extravagant in the cutting. Clean the pot and pack it with new compost, then place the plant back into it. Water and keep out of direct sunlight.

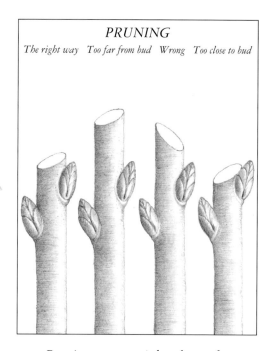

Pruning cuts are trial and error for novice gardeners but soon the correct distance from bud to cut will become clear. Look carefully at these drawings for the right and wrong way.

Stopping is a gentle way to prune plants. Pinch out the growing part to help the plant put out new shoots. The new shoots can also be pinched out to encourage even bushier growth.

ABOVE: A dark large tiled floor is the perfect contrast to the espaliered climbing rose working its way up and across the wall. This rose has been carefully pruned and trained to achieve the shape.

CONSERVATORY STYLE

The Traditional Style

The word "tradition" suggests a reverence for ritual, and for whatever existed in the past. Thus the "pattern" for a traditional conservatory is based on architectural and horticultural details of the Victorian era, a time when the British Empire ruled the world. The current revival of interest in the conservatory reflects a deep yearning and great affection for the ease of life and the family values prevalent in that era. The conservatory was (then) a haven from the regime of the rest of the household. It was a place for leisurely activities—reading, writing

OPPOSITE: White wicker furniture, masses of variously coloured ivy leaf geranium blooms in pots on the central table and around the perimeter of this conservatory combine with a grapevine growing out of the roof to make this a welcoming environment. Note the traditional patterned and tiled floor.

PREVIOUS PAGE: The many fingered leaves of Musanga cecropiodes are often used to provide a shade tree in cocoa and coffee plantations in tropical Africa. Yet they can grow profusely in a conservatory with a tropical temperature level.

letters to friends, taking afternoon tea, entertaining visitors and, of course, caring for the plants.

In contemporary society, the traditional influence is strong. The conservatory is once again the haven—not from the busy household, but from the business world outside its walls. For a few, it is regarded as a status symbol. For most of us, it represents a place to stop and recharge the soul.

There are certain architectural features without which a conservatory cannot be termed "traditional". Scrolled ironwork, curved glazing bars (timber or cast iron), a vaulted ceiling (usually glass), a crested dome or peaked roofline, a tiled or stone floor, an iron central heating grille set in the floor are important details. Any painted surface is white. Panes of glass are often the palest gold, red, green and blue for interesting light effects. Many floors feature tessellated tile designs. Plants are placed in beds around the perimeter and sometimes in the middle of the space, with a tiled path allowing a stroll through the plants.

The decorated image involves tiered shelves for smaller plants, particularly ramblers; decorative plant stands

featuring a flowering plant, and a single plinth displaying a marble bust of a well-known muse or musician and decorative beading are traditional features.

There is a particular style of wicker furniture associated with traditional style. Genuine wicker is softer than cane, and woven in more decorative forms, and when left in its natural colour or painted white, is undeniably reminiscent of the elegance of the Victorian era. The wicker chairs are very comfortable, especially when cushions fill the seat area. Usually, the chair or sofa legs are also entwined with wicker. The table is either round or square and not too large, seating four comfortably. (More is a crowd in the conservatory.) A white linen cloth, edged with embroidery and lace, covers the tabletop.

The traditional planting scheme is less defined, though tall palms in glazed pots, orchids in decorative jardinières, geraniums, fuchsias and maidenhair ferns are common.

To capture the spirit, visit some fine examples of the period. There are often guided tours of famous privately owned gardens with conservatories. Contact the historical society in your region.

Plan for a traditional conservatory

This is designed in the true British tradition. For northern hemisphere readers, plant
this scheme in a south-facing conservatory. For southern hemisphere readers,
plant in a north-facing situation. The scheme involves planting in the ground around
the perimeter, with a central seating and table arrangement. The floor is designed
with contrasting black and white hard-wearing tiles. The view above is of the
lower right-hand section of the scheme.

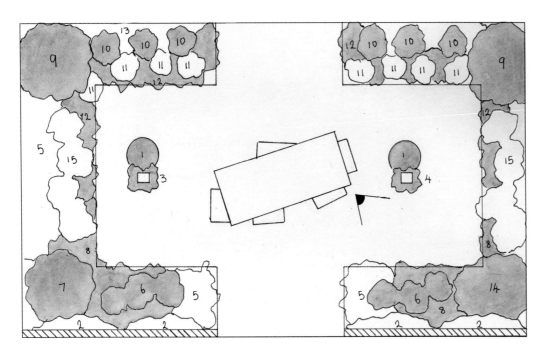

Key to planting scheme

1. *Clivia miniata* (Kaffir lily)
2. *Camellia sasanqua* (Camellia)
3. *Lapageria rosea* (Chilean bell flower)
4. *Trachelospermum jasminoides* (Chinese star jasmine)
5. *Aspidistra elatior* (Aspidistra)
6. *Fuchsia* cv. (Fuchsia)
7. *Fatsia japonica* (Japanese aralia, Castor oil plant)
8. *Saxifraga stolonifera* (Mother of thousands)
9. *Plumbago auriculata* (Cape Leadwort)
10. *Fuchsia* cv. (Standard form)
11. *Azalea indica* cv. (Azalea)
12. *Helxine soleirolii* (Baby's tears, Mind-your-own-business)
13. *Asplenium bulbiferum* (Mother spleenwort)
14. *Nerium oleander* 'Alba' (Oleander)
15. *Pelargonium* cv. (Pelargonium)
➤ Shows area of scheme illustrated.

The intention of this scheme is to create a genteel and cheerful mood in the conservatory. The plants chosen are a mixture of easy-to-grow plants such as fuchsias and the delicate *Lapageria rosea*. The room is approached from the house through double-glazed French doors situated opposite another pair of French doors which lead out to the garden. The design leads either left or right, enabling the visitor to stroll past the plants.

It is a relatively simple scheme which involves placing most of the plants in beds around the perimeter. Consider incorporating an automatic watering system at ground level. The flooring is paved with black and white hard-wearing ceramic tiles—you may prefer stone paving slabs.

As always when planning a planting scheme, consider the theme. Do you want to use plants which are all pink, blue, lilac or red? Or do you prefer to mix and match? The answer to this affects the decision concerning the style of fabric for the seat covers. Choose a fabric which is hard-wearing and easy to keep clean and is of a pattern which tones with the planting scheme. Using a red and orange fabric, say, when all of the plants are pale pink, will not be easy on the eye. It is preferable to keep all painted surfaces white.

The placement of fuchsias and ivy geranium (*Pelargonium* sp.) in hanging baskets is cleverly away from general foot traffic and the seating area. (In summertime, it is a good idea to spray the fuchsias with a fine mist to keep the plants in excellent condition. Spring is the time to prune, cutting the plants back so that they will bloom abundantly in summer.)

For the truly traditional touch, there is an aspidistra (*Aspidistra elatior*) and a beautiful camellia (*Camellia sasanqua*) espaliered against the solid wall. More plants in tubs can easily be added to the scheme if you like to create a busier style.

ABOVE: *Simplicity is the key to the success of this conservatory designed as an extra living space. The floor boards have been limed to match the lightness of the chairs; white shade blinds cover the glass ceiling and sheer white drapes are at each window ready to provide shade if necessary. The height of the two potted weeping figs* (Ficus benjamina) *adds a dramatic element.*

LEFT: *In a traditional mode, ready for an intimate dinner. Dark shade cloth blinds are rolled to either side of the room, and its glass roof features a central opening mechanism for ventilation. Lush tall ivy geranium plants are placed at either side, with* Stephanotis *winding its way over a cross-bar. To the right foreground is* Sparrmania africana.

The Mostly Fern-filled Conservatory

One of the most sensational fern-filled conservatories in the northern hemisphere is at Kibble Palace in the Botanic Gardens, Glasgow, Scotland. Here you will see the exquisite beauty of a forest-like environment created by towering tropical tree ferns. The New York Botanical Garden Conservatory, located in the Bronx in New York, America, also features a magnificent collection of ferns, mingling with a profusion of orchids.

OPPOSITE: Gloriously green is this collection of ivy (Hedera helix), *lacy fern* (Asparagus setaceus), *a shield fern* (Polystichum) *and Baby's tears* (Helxine), *a compact creeper which makes excellent ground cover. It loves humidity and grows rapidly in warm conservatories. Almost on the ground is* Selaginella.

In England, a renewed interest in temperate plants was responsible for the construction of the Temperate House at Kew Gardens in the 1860s. Ferns were a major focal point of this temperate conservatory and many people adopted the idea, creating conservatories devoted to just ferns, hence the development of the word "fernery". The ferns were planted mostly in large pots, cleverly placed behind large boulders in artificial rockeries. The haphazard form created by the outline of the rocks led traditional design away from straight, tiled pathways to a more rambling path between ferns. From this time onward, it became acceptable to experiment with new planting designs.

More and more early botanists were returning from far flung shores with exotic species, keen to display their treasures. The ideal place for them was in the fernery, its humid conditions a replica of their natural environment.

There is no doubt that ferns are graceful. Their fronds are too enticing not to touch. To grow ferns successfully in a conservatory, it is important to plant them on the shady side of the room, and to ensure that the soil is moist and the air quite humid. Do not overwater—watch the roots for signs of rot. The glorious tree fern *Dicksonia antarctica* grows to a height of 6 feet (180cm) and its delicate fronds spread beautifully if planted with sufficient space around it. Growth is slow but patience is rewarded with a splendid specimen. This fern grows in both warm and cool conservatories if the same shady and humid conditions exist. Personally, I adore the shape and texture of the fronds of maidenhair fern (*Adiantum cuneatum*) and the glorious staghorn fern (*Platycerium superbum*).

Plan for a fernery

This illustration is of a plan perfect for re-creating the cool lushness of a fernery.
A humid shady space is necessary for these ferns to flourish throughout the year,
providing the conservatory owner with a green landscape to treasure.
The view above is of the lower left-hand corner of the scheme.

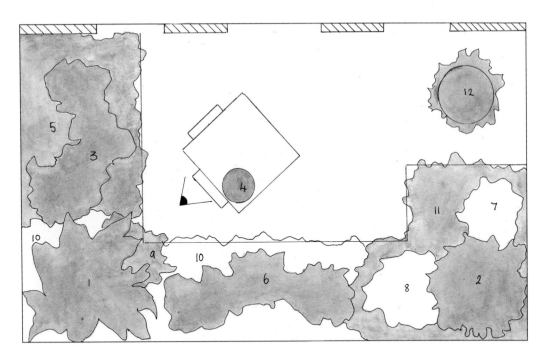

This plan suits a small conservatory; one that receives little heat from sunlight. Most of the plants shown here are best grown in soil beds. To achieve this, build a garden bed the length of the solid wall, and approximately 3 feet (90cm) wide. Fill with a high quality soil mixture. Build another of the same width along the length of a side wall. Note that the plants must be placed away from direct sunlight. If you cannot build such a bed, then large pots will do equally well. Be sure to group the pots together to achieve the same mass foliage effect.

In the corner, as a focal point, is the magnificent tree fern *Dicksonia antarctica*, which will grow to tower over the other ferns and the *Fatsia japonica* directly in front of it. Clever use of space is everything in a small area, and this plan allows for an intimate dining area without it appearing too enclosed. A mixture of soft greenery—the bird's nest fern (*Asplenium nidus*) and ribbon fern (*Pteris cretica*)—with the aspidistra (*Aspidistra elatior*) will be wonderful in this situation. Ferns have such interesting shapes and contrasting foliage, when grouped together they create a wonderful tableau.

It is a good idea to fill the area between ferns with a damp moss of some type to help prevent moisture loss. Ferns hanging from baskets will add another dimension to this small space. Try *Protasparagus densiflorus* 'Sprengeri' and *Nephrolepis exaltata* 'Elegantissima' in their own area, as a complement to the rest of the plants.

The Conservatory in Winter

During the harshness of any winter, particularly a northern winter, the type of heating system you have installed will be very important to your plants' survival. Winter is the key time for the conservatory; it is a time for wintering over plants from the outdoors; a time to nurture those plants which are rare and special to your collection. As a leisure space, the conservatory plays another role—just as important—as a place to sit and watch the chilling mist descend upon the surrounding garden while you feel warm and snug, yet surrounded by blooming foliage that, by nature's rights, ought not to be blooming.

OPPOSITE: Visual interest is provided by decorative elements in this winter conservatory. A statue in repose, an animal sculpture, a small bust on the glass-topped table and fancy candle holders in style with the hanging light fitting—all are at home among the weeping fig tree (Ficus benjamina), the Pacific Island shrub (Polyscias filicifolia), the mother fern (Asplenium bulbiferum) by the glass topped table, and ivy (Hedera sp). Note that as much light as possible is allowed to enter the conservatory to stimulate plant growth.

The main point to remember is that in a heated conservatory you must choose plants which prefer a dry, centrally heated space throughout winter. Try to maintain a temperature of 65°F (16°C) by day during this time, and a relatively medium level of humidity. Avoid sudden temperature changes, so watch the exterior doors! Make sure friends and family close them after themselves, and close the windows at night when the temperature drops. Your house's heating system will take over at night.

The sun during winter contains a lot less heat than during the fierce summer days, so do not count on it warming the conservatory quite as much as during summer. Place those plants which need more light near the windows in this type of space, and those plants which prefer cooler areas in the shady part, away from the heating units.

What to grow is always a tricky question. The plants you choose will depend upon your budget for heating. If money is not a problem then your winter conservatory can look brilliant, alive with climbers and rare species but do remember that all plants have their periods of slow growth during winter time, even though you may try to trick

them with unnatural conditions. This is particularly so with species of cacti. Plants like the hardy annuals, some bulbs and some of the hardier palms will survive in the winter environment, as does the camellia or the gorgeous shrub *Fatsia japonica*.

If you intend to keep the conservatory cool in winter, then try varieties of grapes which actually like the shelter of an unheated conservatory during the winter months. The trailing vine of a grape looks striking even when it is not covered in foliage.

The lowest winter temperature for many tropical and subtropical plants hovers between 45°F (7°C) and 50°F (10°C), so it is best to ask the plant supplier for details about heat and humidity requirements of individual species. The less hardy tropical plants, such as orchids, require a temperature of at least 65°F (16°C) and high humidity. If you want to continue growing these through winter be prepared for high heating bills, and a steamy conservatory. You could create a smaller area of the main conservatory and devote this space to these species, adding heated lights above individual plants and screening them from drafts.

Plan for a winter conservatory

This illustration is of a plan for an oasis of green, one to make the spirit soar during dark winter months—wherever you are in the world. There is a variety of leaf textures and shades of foliage to make the room extremely interesting to the owner and visitor alike. The view here is of the right-hand side wall of the scheme.

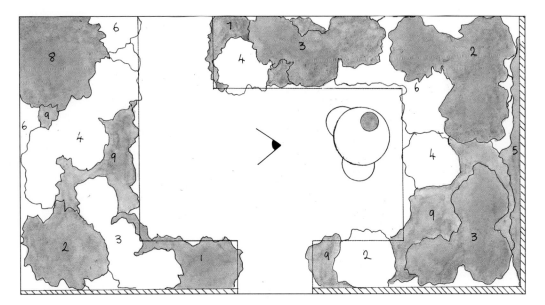

Key to planting scheme

1. *Aspidistra elatior* (Aspidistra)
2. *Howea forsterana* (Kentia palm)
3. *Rhapis excelsa* (Lady palm)
4. *Fatsia japonica* (Japanese aralia, Castor oil plant)
5. *Cissus antarctica* (Kangaroo vine)
6. *Adiantum capillus-veneris* (Maidenhair fern)
7. *Pteris cretica* (Ribbon fern)
8. *Ficus benjamina* (Weeping fig)
9. *Spathiphyllum wallisii* (White sails, Peace lily)
➤ Shows area of scheme illustrated.

To have such a splendid opportunity to plant a winter conservatory is a challenge. This scheme is of palms and ferns, using the textures of foliage to create the interest. This plan requires a shaded, moist, and protected location within the conservatory, and if you live in a cold climate which has freezing winters, you will need to ensure that the heating system is accurate. Too much heat will be disastrous. In warm climates, you will probably only need heat during the winter nights.

Enter from the house to behold a central, paved, living space with round table and folding chairs surrounded by planted beds at ground level. The basic idea is to mass ground covers, adding taller plants and hanging baskets for further effect. Most of the planting is in beds, located at ground level, edged with tiles. The flooring in this conservatory must be waterproof—stone paving laid in an interesting pattern would look terrific, like a forest path—with good drainage as ferns and palms need watering and general care and attention. Regularly remove dead fronds, and check for pests and disease. You may like to hose and sweep the area free of fallen bits of greenery.

The aspidistra, maidenhair and ribbon ferns, plus *Spathiphyllum wallisii*, are used to create a mass of ground cover and will be glorious once they have taken root thoroughly.

The kentia palm (*Howea forsterana*) is an elegant species, slow growing but certainly a splendid sight when its large palmate leaves are fully grown. Do not attempt to grow this species in hot, dry conditions. It will suffer, the tips of its leaves turning brown at the edges. Plant the palms close to a light source, and in the cooler part of the conservatory.

To add a sense of drama at night in the palm conservatory, place spotlights at ground level so that the beam highlights the palm leaves, creating shadowy effects. The ground covers will also come into focus. Hanging baskets for this conservatory could be planted with the pretty *Nephrolepis exaltata* 'Hillii' and *Hedera helix,* a lovely climbing ivy. (Be sure to place this in a cooler area of the conservatory as warm conditions make it attractive to red spider mite.)

The Cottage Conservatory

There is nothing more delightful than walking into a room filled with the fragrance of flowers. The cottage effect is one to plan carefully, as you would in an outdoor garden, because of all of the designs the cottage demands more plant material and more of your personality. This style is ideally suited to an enclosed area such as a conservatory and is composed of smaller, unpretentious plants, lively in shape and texture. Old-fashioned flowers will add a familiar, decorative element to the theme.

To achieve the effect, plant the species close together to create a profusion of blooms and foliage. Begin from the ground upwards, making use of three-tiered planting stands, plinths, and built-in benches. Climbers are essential in any cottage scheme. You may like to add small sculptures amid the flowers, standing on carved plinths, set on the table or hidden between the plant beds or containers. Architectural features such as latticework or painted metal archways (up and over which you could train a clematis variety) add a certain romantic cottage look. Planned carefully, the structures would not intrude upon the conservatory itself. They would become part of the "look".

It is essential that the furniture reflect this cottage look. Small flower print fabric-covered cushions, tablecloths edged with lace, wicker or iron-lace chairs and tables, simple wooden plinths or three-tiered plant stands are worth considering. Avoid slick flooring and try for the stone "crazy-paving" look. A comfortable look is the aim here.

Flowers such as roses, clove-scented pinks, primroses, hydrangeas, hollyhocks, mignonette and lavender are ideal for this theme. Use sunny areas of the room to grow tender flowering annuals and perennials. Above all, remember that simplicity of design and planting will make this a successful theme.

LEFT: A seeming jumble of greenery greets the visitor in this gorgeous cottage-style conservatory. A grapevine is trained to trail above beds planted with a wide variety of foliage and flowering plants. A red geranium hangs from the vine; a Pteris *fern, English variegated ivy and a magnificent variegated* Pisonia *feature strongly in the crowd.*

Plan for a cottage conservatory

The mix of plants used in this plan will bring great joy to anyone keen to create a
cottage-style mood in their conservatory. It is imaginative in its combinations,
and planned to provide either flower or foliage interest throughout the year.
Above is a view of the lower wall shown in the scheme.

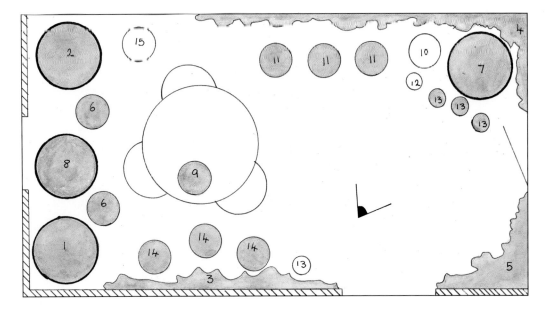

Even in a conservatory, a successful cottage garden scheme requires care and attention. The scheme's success depends less upon good design lines than on achieving a multi-layered profusion of interesting plants. This plan requires a light-filled conservatory, and the owner to be prepared to care for the plants on a regular basis.

It involves a rectangular space, entered from the house along the longer wall, over which trails a giant potato vine. The exit to the garden is to the right, allowing the rest of the space to be given over to plants and a dining table setting. This is a really pretty plan, with Cape jasmine (*Gardenia jasminoides*), morning glory (*Ipomoea tricolor*) and Madagascar jasmine (*Stephanotis floribunda*) trailing above and around hydrangea (*Hydrangea macrophylla*), Cape primrose (*Streptocartus* x *hybridus*) and varieties of fuchsia (*Fuchsia* sp.). The addition of quite a few hanging baskets trailing a variety of fuchsias and ivies will add to the cottage appearance. Choose plants which complement the shade of plants in the main space, as there is nothing worse than looking up from a gentle lilac, blue or pink scheme to behold bright red and orange blooms looming down upon your head.

If your conservatory has a glass roof which gets more than its fair share of sun, you may have to install shade blinds to prevent the more delicate plants from shrivelling up in the heat and glare. Be vigilant in watering and pruning the vines and fuchsias to produce the absolute best extravagant display from each plant.

ABOVE: *A delightful pink azalea, an oleander in bud and small scented leaf geraniums feature with the small classic-style statue in this country conservatory.*

LEFT: *Comfortable furniture, laid for a casual meal, sits beneath a canopy of a wonderful climbing grapevine which is loaded with blossom in the height of the season.*

Cacti in the conservatory

This is one of the most interesting plant species, and sure to be a conversation piece when friends visit. The cactus plant and its cute flowers have developed a cult status many now happily bloom on the office desk, being quite at home in the warmth of a dry, air-conditioned office environment. These plants have a weird appearance, either looking like smooth stones or prickly hedgehogs and pin cushions. Their bulky stems hold all the water a plant needs during periods of drought. The pickles are a natural defence mechanism against natural predators. When the small bright flowers blooms, these plants take on a character of their own.

Cacti exist in a series of separate groups characterized by their shape and appearance. Some types grow tall; others remain squat, hairy and prickly. The miniature varieties make a terrific impression when planted *en masse* in a rectangular container. They make good conservatory plants as they can grow steadily without too much attention, provided the atmosphere is hot, dry, and sunny. They do have a winter period when growth slows, but a good watering before spring encourages the formation of the small and vibrant flowers.

Remember to take more care of the *Mammillaria* group because fungal rot is inclined to attack this species.

In the planting scheme opposite, the entrance is from the house through a wide double doorway, leading the eye to the bench located directly opposite. Here the cacti are displayed as the focal point of the room. Larger plants are strategically placed as a contrast to the delicacy of the Christmas cactus (*Schlumbergera* x *buckleyi*), whose varieties feature white, magenta, pink and orange flowers. The delightful *Rhipsalidopsis gaertneri* and the amazing *Kalanchoe blossfeldiana* 'Emma Lord'. Magnificent against this focal point are the two Spanish bayonets (*Yucca aloifolia*) and the familiar European fan palm (*Chamaerops humilis*). Further cactus species can be added to the bench display, depending upon the time of year. Hedgehog cactus (*Echinocactus*) is a large, barrel-shaped plant with tiny flowers and a lot of prickles. One of the largest genera of cacti is the *Mammillaria* which features lots of small long-lasting flowers— watch out for the delicate *M. plumosa* which is a mass of feathery white spines. The cactus Pachycereus is a larger, tree-like plant with a short trunk which requires plenty of light.

This is a design plan with which you can have fun establishing your personality in the conservatory.

ABOVE: A wonderful display of many varieties of the cactus family.

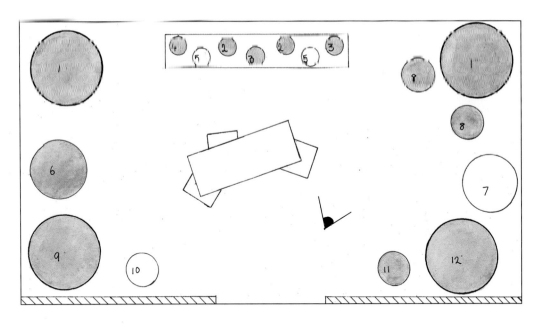

Key to planting scheme

1. *Yucca aloifolia* (Spanish bayonet)
2. *Schlumbergera x buckleyi* (Christmas cactus)
3. *Schlumbergera* 'Christmas joy' (Christmas cactus)
4. *Rhipsalidopsis gaertneri* (Easter cactus)
5. *Kalanchoe blossfeldiana* 'Emma Lord'
6. *Beaucarnea recurvata* (Pony-tail plant)
7. *Crassula ovata* (Jade tree)
8. *Sansevieria trifasciata* 'Laurentii' (Mother-in-law's tongue)
9. *Chamaerops humilis* (European fan palm)
10. *Dizygotheca elegantissima* (False aralia)
11. *Dracaena marginata* 'Variegata' (Madagascar dragon tree)
12. *Cordyline australis* (New Zealand cabbage tree)

> Shows area of scheme illustrated.

Below is a view of the top right-hand corner of the scheme.

The Palm Conservatory

Here we have the image that, for most people, comes to mind when the word conservatory is spoken.

Palms are magnificent, elegant, and are deserving of all forms of appreciation. There is a wide variety of shapes and sizes in this genus, ranging from the dwarf palm Cocos to the familiar kentia palm (*Howea forsterana*) and Phoenix palm (*Phoenix roebelenii*).

For those who have visited the splendid Palm House at the Royal Gardens at Kew, England, the true spirit of a palm conservatory will always be present. Founded by Prince Frederick, father of George III, this imposing structure was built of cast and wrought iron, the frame resting on a stone base. The central dome is 65 feet (20m) high and displays the tallest palms in the unique collection.

I recently walked to the viewing platform via the spiral staircase to properly view the palms in their full glory. The humidity level is reminiscent of a hot night in Singapore. (But how satisfying to gaze upon the palms.) It is possible to achieve a small scale version of this with a well-planned conservatory, and a heating and ventilation system that will ensure the correct level of humidity.

Palms like a moist, humid environment and although they grow reasonably well in shade, palms prefer to be placed in the lighter areas of a room.

It is their glossy green foliage which, for me, makes them the most appealing indoor plant. They are quite at home in a well-drained pot or container, and this also makes it easy to move them around the conservatory according to the seasons.

LEFT: Standing grandly in the corner is a fine example of the Washingtonia palm with its fat bowl and inter-locking leaf base. To the left in a pot is Calathea *and to the right, the touch of pink is a lobster claw (*Vriesia, *one of the bromeliad species).*

Plan for a palm conservatory

Illustrated above is the view of the planting scheme looking towards the seating area for two people. Simplicity is the key in this plan, with plenty of light for the sensitive palms.

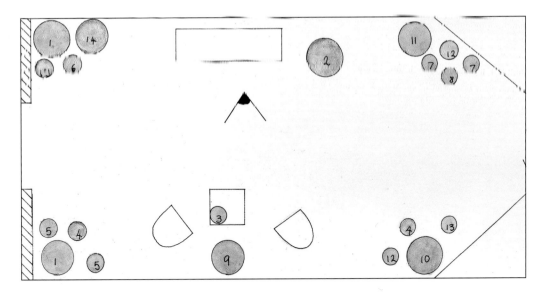

Grouping palms in pots and containers is an effective way to display these plants. This design is based on a large rectangular conservatory, with the entrance from the house located to take visitors right through the collection to the garden exit. Good light is essential, as is heat during the chill of winter. The plan creates a light and airy atmosphere, with collections of palms at each corner.

A seat for three is placed centrally along one wall, and two chairs are directly opposite. Fabric covered cushions allow a personal design statement as well as providing comfort on what really ought to be pieces of wicker, not wrought-iron or cane, furniture. A tiled or stone-paved floor completes the nostalgic scene, perhaps with an oriental rug laid at the foot of the seating.

The larger pots contain kentia palms (*Howea forsterana*) and the wonderful parlour palm (*Chamaedorea elegans*) with its long and feathery fronds. Flaming sword (*Vriesia splendens*) is a lovely addition in here, as is the peace lily (*Spathiphyllum wallisii*) with its sturdy, glossy green leaves and white blooms on slender stems. New varieties of the latter have fragrant blossoms but the lovely foliage is the main attraction.

The Entrance Conservatory

This is a wonderful idea for creating a buffer zone between the exterior garden and the interior of the house. As you approach the house, what better sight could there be than that of an elegant structure filled with pretty flowers and foliage? Many homes are designed without a hallway and with the front door opening immediately into the living room. The addition of a conservatory will solve this space problem. The porch area does not have to be especially large, but should be wide enough to place the plants to each side, away from the central traffic area leading from both doorways.

OPPOSITE: A gentle profusion of wisteria foliage greets the visitor to this entrance conservatory. Peering out from the large pot is a purple Cape primrose (Streptocarpus). Plants are massed to either side, leaving a walkway.

It is best to keep the style of the addition in keeping with the style of the front of the house—if the house is brick, then a brick base with either timber or iron window frames (depending upon the type of window frames used for the front of the house) is recommended. A glazed roof is ideal for letting in sunlight and adding a greater feeling of height to the area. Stone slabs, quarry tiles or hard-wearing ceramic tiles are essential for the floor in what is a well-used "foot traffic" area. The classic entrance floor uses black and white tiles in a harlequin pattern—a style that always evokes images of a more genteel era. Do choose a non-slip finish, and ensure that there is a slight slope to a drain for rainwater which inevitably builds up in such areas.

A modern home deserves an addition in the modern idiom, so consider this design element carefully before beginning construction. There is a variety of exciting modern designs readily available as glass and metal manufacturers develop tougher yet flexible products—all it takes is a little imagination to create a unique addition. Some types of modern glass are manufactured with insulating and reflecting layers built in to shut out the heat and glare in daytime, and yet conserve heat during the night.

The choice of style will, to some extent, dictate the choice of plants for this area. It is not advisable to choose plants that suffer in a draft because, no matter how careful you are, there will be a draft every time the door is opened. Look for hardy plants with interesting shapes and great foliage. Small weeping tree shapes are good for corners; place small groupings of pot plants at ground level for a dramatic effect. A last hint: place an attractive container near the front door for wet umbrellas!

Plan for an entrance conservatory

Imagine this entrance space attached to the front of a classic brick-fronted house, its side
walls a combination of white-painted timber glazing bars sitting on a low brick wall.
The single front door is solid and also painted white. Open the door and step inside to behold
a mass of joyful blooms and foliage. This is the ideal link between the exterior and
the interior. Above is a view of the centre wall to the top of the scheme.

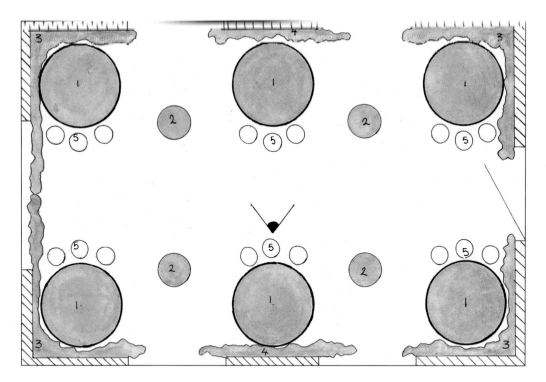

The concept for the plan is formal, with major planting to either side of the space. The focal point is provided by the fabulous foliage of the weeping fig (*Ficus benjamina*) placed in a row along each side wall. At the base is a small group of *Cyclamen persicum*, fuchsia, busy Lizzie (*Impatiens*), Madonna lily (*Lilium candidum*) and poinsettia (*Euphorbia pulcherrima*). Adding even more pleasure are hanging baskets of *Nephrolepis exaltata* 'Bostoniensis'. The presence of the wonderful fast-growing Kangaroo vine (*Cissus antarctica*) indicates a note of informality creeping into the scene.

The scheme is interesting as it allows for a seasonal variation. The tubs and pots can be changed at will, enabling a different flower and foliage theme to be introduced after one season's growth. Pale flowering plants may be replaced by those of a brighter shade; plain green leafy plants replaced by those with a variegated leaf pattern. It is important to keep the height of a plant like the weeping fig because the branches create a sense of privacy, screening the area from intrusive eyes. They also provide shade for plants at ground level. This space is ideal as an overnight home for some of the more delicate plants usually grown outside, especially during winter months. (You are more likely to take notice of them if they are inside!)

Consider, too, the type of lighting needed in this area. Placing spotlights along a central ceiling line, with the spots highlighting special plants, is effective. Spotlights hidden in the ground pots, lighting the plants from below, create a dramatic tableau without costing too much money. Consult an electrician as to the correct wiring and type of spotlight suitable for this situation.

ABOVE: *This is a light-filled entance conservatory leading from the back garden into the house. A* magnificent weeping fig tree (Ficus benjamina) *in a terracotta pot, a creeping jasmin* (Jasminum polyanthum) *which will bloom with masses of flowers in season, and the sucker leadwort* (Plumbago) *in the urn in the foreground maintain the garden-like atmosphere.*

RIGHT: *Terracotta tiles will wear well under constant foot traffic. The fabric parasol with its bamboo frame is a portable solution to the shade problem. Hanging down is a golden flowered* Lantana camara *and a marigold plant.*

The Fruit and Vegetable Conservatory

The origins of this type of conservatory are steeped in history; the earliest can be traced back to Roman times, and it later developed as the European orangerie.

The orangerie was a basic enclosure built as a means of protecting precious citrus trees and vegetable plants (brought back from conquered lands) from the harshness of the northern European winters. These early enclosures were built of timber or stone and brick, with ventilation; and the horticulturists at that time burned candles inside to provide heat and occasionally lit small contained fires that would last through the night.

Glazing began to be used in these structures in the 17th century, generally along the wall sited facing full sunlight. These enclosures were simple buildings

LEFT: A simple contemporary setting in a stark environment is brightened by the orange of the ornamental citrus trees in large pots. Plenty of sunlight has proved fortuitous for these trees as the abundance of healthy fruit shows.

but with the development of the manufacturing industry in the 18th and 19th centuries and mass production of glass and glazing bars, the idea caught on throughout Europe and more decorative elements appeared in the design. Architects enjoyed the challenge of balancing the elements of light, heat and humidity to create the ideal conservatory for growing plants inside. They saw this structure as a means of showcasing their talent for the fantastic.

The Restoration period saw further development of the conservatory/greenhouse in Great Britain. Inside these buildings, orange and lemon tree varieties were joined by grapevines and truly exotic edibles such as the pineapple plant. This edible plant aspect still appeals to conservatory owners. To be able to pick a ripe orange from your own tree is quite an achievement in a climate where the citrus tree does not naturally grow. A heat-controlled environment will produce, with good fortune, a fine crop of cultivated tender varieties. Which temperature will produce the best envi-

ronment is debatable, but not much growth will be achieved if the temperature drops below 55°F (12°C). Not only is this type of conservatory practical as the cost of out-of-season fruits soar, but it is also attractive.

Citrus species need tending, with a special regard to pests and diseases. If you want to shape a miniature tree in a particular way, you must prune it regularly. Some of the classic shapes look terrific when grouped together, or added as a decorative touch to a group of furniture. Planting small ornamental fruit trees in large ornate pots or containers makes it easier to ensure that the plant receives an even amount of sunlight and night-time warmth. You can also move them around the conservatory as the seasons change. When buying fruit or vegetable plants, look for varieties that will do well in this indoor environment. Experiment with figs, grape vines, peaches, apricots, and melons. Vegetables that do well include small tomatoes, green and red peppers (capsicums), eggplants (aubergines) and zucchinis (courgettes). Good luck!

Plan for a fruit and vegetable conservatory

Above is a view of the top right-hand section of the scheme.

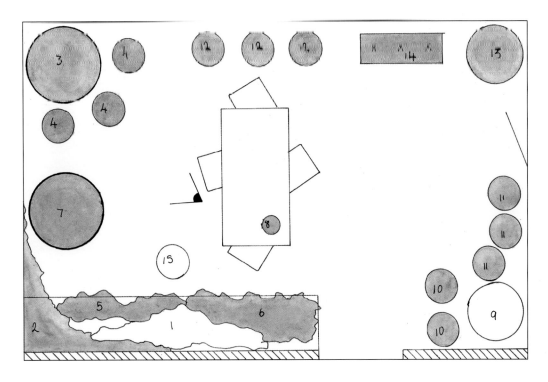

Most of the planting in this scheme is in containers and pots, except for the corner bed of peach and grapevine, parsley and chives. The pepper (*Capsicum annuum*) and eggplant /aubergine (*Solanum melongena*) are seasonal varieties and as you see can perch prettily on a large table. Strawberry plants can be grown in a strawberry pyramid in an oak barrel or hanging in a pocketed basket for greater visual effect. Construct a shelf and situate it in the sunlight for tomatoes, eggplant (aubergine), green and red peppers (capsicum) with winter lettuce growing in the ground underneath or in a large deep tray on a workbench. The hardy lemon (*Citrus limon* 'Meyer') and the African lily (*Agapanthus praecox* ssp. *orientalis*) can be taken outside to a sheltered patio position during summer. Attractive blooms can be planted beneath the cumquat (*Fortunella margarita*) and rosemary (*Rosmarinus officinalis*). Petunias are a pretty seasonal addition, and *Convolvulus mauritanicus* will make a wonderful permanent splash under the rosemary.

DECORATIVE FEATURES

Mixing flowers and furniture

The focus in a conservatory is on the beauty of the plants, yet these blooms also provide a splendid setting against which the inspired decorator can create a series of small and dramatic tableaus. The shape and style of the room will, to a certain extent, dictate the style of the furnishings and the fixtures you choose, but within these boundaries there is still tremendous scope.

Source furniture that will last in damp conditions, and choose furnishing

OPPOSITE: A collection of decorative items for the modern conservatory includes a pair of French antique iron gates (which could be imaginatively used in a design) and an antique, tiered iron plant stand. Other essentials: the green enamelled watering can and the gardening boots for when the floor is chilly and damp; fabrics with a floral theme for cushions and tablecloths, a traditional Lloyd Loom wicker chair and table and small dining table and a collection of pots and containers in a choice of shapes and textures. Do not forget the gardening gloves.

PREVIOUS PAGE: Classical columns and an elaborately carved mirror frame star against the red brickwall. The lushness of large palms in glazed pots is the perfect foil to the coolness of the beige and white furnishings. This corner is an ideal hideaway from the outside world.

accessories such as cushions and blinds with a water-proof finish to prevent the growth of mould in damp conditions. I would suggest that to put a glorious antique lacquered or waxed table and chair set in a damp environment would result in irreparable damage to the pieces. Wooden furniture swells when left for long periods in damp conditions, and splits when left in a warm environment. Varnish dries and peels too frequently in this situation, too.

Furniture made of iron, painted or baked with a permanent sealant, is ideal. So is cane or wicker, both of which are hard-wearing materials and will last a good many years if looked after properly. Should the paint chip, touch it up immediately with one of the useful kits now available at hardware stores.

Brand new furniture will look a little formal when first placed in the room but if you choose a combination of new and old, then the effect you want to create will happen more easily. Second-hand furniture stores and antique markets are a haven for seekers of Victorian plants stands, decorative urns and pots. An antique plate or saucer looks lovely underneath a pot plant, adding even more colour to a scheme. (Make sure it is not an extremely rare plate!)

THE CONSERVATORY AS A DINING ROOM

These days, the use of a conservatory has become two-fold. It is no longer a place just for growing and displaying new plants. It has become a room designed for living. More often than not, a space especially for dining. To be able to eat in the conservatory, surrounded by the fragrance of a variety of plants, is a special experience and one to be valued. On a day in early spring or late autumn, when the sun is shining and the day is clear but cold, the conservatory becomes a second garden. You can enjoy the feeling of almost being in the garden, yet being warm and comfortable.

The design of the room will dictate the shape of the dining table. A long, rectangular room will be best suited by a table of the same proportions. The same design rule applies to an octagonal shaped room — choose either a round table or smaller, square table for this situation.

Where you place the setting is decided by the foot traffic plan. Be sure to plan where you want the table and chairs prior to planning the planting scheme. If you decide to locate plants around the exterior of the room, then the centre of the room is best for a seating arrangement. But, if the centre of the room is in the middle of a pathway leading from the inside of the house to the doors leading to the garden, that may not be such a good plan. Try to place the setting to the left or right of that traffic area as it will, in the long run, be more convenient. Also consider where the sun comes into the room, remembering that sunlight fades furnishing fabrics. Perhaps you may like to include a storage space for these items nearby.

Think also about the heating system — the table and chair arrangement can be used to hide the radiator pipes.

On the floor, use hard-wearing rugs in that suit the scheme. Or you may like to use rattan matting just for the floor area around the table and chair setting — it is less hard on the feet.

The space for dining should not be vast. It is the one area in the room that must be intimate. So consider placing the table and chairs amidst a grouping

ABOVE: A good decorative idea for a table top: plant a container with a miniature leaf ivy and train it to encircle a wire frame. It will look more wonderful each season.

of foliage and flowers, leaving enough space for guests to move easily in and out of their chairs. Think carefully about the type of plant to place around the table as too much human contact may damage the leaves or flowers.

Let the flowers provide the basic colour in the dining area. Plants are like the furniture in the conservatory and they can be moved around at the change of season. So it is best to start with strong basics and then add the accessories — table cloth, napkins, candle-holder and candles, crockery and cutlery. Look for shapes and colours to match the surrounding flowers. Cushion covers can be plain with a floral trim, or floral with a single colour trim.

Soft colours create harmony in a mixed colour area, yet if your planting scheme features strong red, green, yellow and orange, then look for similar tones of those strong colours in furnishing accessories. One pale colour, such as cream, is an alternative to consider, especially if you have chosen a natural wicker table and chair set. If your conservatory is of a modern style, avoid using traditional large floral printed fabrics and choose instead modern abstract floral patterns.

Most importantly, keep to the one decorating style. If you choose a Victorian replica, then decorate it in true Victorian style. If you have chosen a modern style, then the same decorating idiom is to apply.

Take inspiration from nature's colour schemes — and let the flowers be the focal point.

THE CONSERVATORY AS A SECRET PLACE

In such a room, plants are the focal point and any furniture is hidden behind large plants. A comfortable sofa and small side table for books are all that are necessary in this intimate space. A small chair for a guest or two can be added. Such spaces are best created to one end, be it in a large or small conservatory. Place decorative screens to hide the furniture. Look for unique screens — either the hand-painted Chinese type, or those hung with gathered fabric. Cane and basketweave screens are also good as decoration.

Use tall palms in large, heavy pots to create a discreet barrier between you and the rest of the space.

PLANT FURNITURE

To make the most of a smaller garden space (which a conservatory is) staggered shelving or staging is a clever way to achieve a mass of colour and/or foliage at different levels. Construction is usually of timber or wrought iron; staging is best tiered against the edges of a conservatory, against a wall or the glass. Some free-standing tiered units also look effective, especially if full of smaller pots. Painted pieces look best in dark green or white, merging with the foliage. Natural iron or cane look best left in their natural state.

For palms, large oriental-style pots are perfect, especially when a group of three or four is placed in a corner. Smaller pots can be grouped in larger numbers for effect. Using pots with plants at different heights and differing stages of growth creates more visual effect. Too many plants at the same height merely creates a wall of foliage with ugly gaps between the growth and the pot.

PLANT ACCESSORIES

Pots for plants are currently manufactured in a wide array of shapes and sizes. Look for hand-made and hand-painted pots and planters for an individual look; or try being creative yourself. Here is a good idea that can easily be done by the home craftsperson: All you need is one clay pot, some craft glue and a piece of colourful thick weave fabric cut to the shape of the pot. Carefully glue the fabric to the pot, making sure you turn the edges of the fabric over at the top and bottom of the pot. You may like to hem the fabric prior to applying. A group display of these fabric-covered pots is effective, especially when planted with African violets or primulas in a range of colours to match the fabric. The best thing about this idea is that you can change the fabric with the seasons and the style.

Plastic pots are ideal for new seedlings but as they grow, transfer them into clay pots which are better for the plant's well-being as they absorb water.

Buy a pair of good quality secateurs for pruning. Oil them regularly. Create a storage space for a collection of pots and tools, ideally under a work bench.

PERFECT PLANTS

Plants for the conservatory

The following comprehensive list is divided into groups which will easily allow you to choose the types of plants suitable for the mood you wish to create in the conservatory.

In the relatively small space, it is wise to establish a single theme, being careful not to mix romantic cottage plants with those of the jungle. Clever placement of a few evergreens provides a good foundation for whichever scheme you choose to follow.

The variety of greens in interesting foliage, massed in an imaginative manner, is wonderful to behold at any time of the year, but especially during the dull winter months. The shape of foliage is also visually exciting — some

OPPOSITE: Daffodils, tulips, gerberas, primulas and hyacinth plants in various household containers make a cheerful grouping on a window ledge.

PREVIOUS PAGE: The interesting variegated foliage of the painted nettle (Coleus blumei) makes a splendid contribution to any conservatory.

look like sharp swords; others have spindly leaves or wide and jagged edges. When placing plants in an area, try to create a contrast of both colour and shape. To be effective, group a few similar plants together, with a few of another type adjacent. Some of the more interesting variegated cultivars have stripes and dots, plus flashes of silver and gold, cream, red and purple on a background of deep or the palest green. Foliage plants do not like direct sunlight so try to place them in the shade.

Look for plants which provide a variety of height, form and colour to ensure success in a scheme — try mixing wall climbers with potted plants placed at different levels. Bushy hanging baskets and plants trailing from wall brackets also provide a different dimension. Versatility is also important. Pots allow you to change the display, useful if one plant needs more heat or light than another.

Consult the plant expert in your region as to which plants are best suited for the type of conservatory garden you wish to establish.

FLOWERING ANNUALS
Calceolaria

Sometimes called slipper flower for their inflated flowers in a range of gaudy hues, *calceolarias* are one of those conservatory plants best purchased just as the first buds open, after which they can be enjoyed for four to six weeks if kept in reasonably bright light and watered frequently. Minimum temperature 50°F (10°C).
C. x *herbeohybrida* annual to 2ft (60cm), many named varieties and strains, mostly mixed hues.

Catharanthus
MADAGASCAR PERIWINKLE

A cheerful, soft shrubby plant, usually treated as an annual, which revels in hot dry conditions. Valuable medicinal drugs, used in cancer treatment, are obtained from this species. Stems are fleshy, leaves shiny, and the starry white, pink or mauve-purple flowers are produced in continuous succession for as long as the weather stays warm. Varieties with flowers darker in the middle are now popular. Sunlight is essential for good flowering. Buy plants in spring or raise from seed in late winter. Minimum temperature 50°F (10°C).

C. roseus to 18in (45cm) high and broadly spreading; flowers to 1 1/2in (4cm) in diameter are borne singly on leafy branch tips.

Eustoma

This pretty annual has recently enjoyed a great upsurge in popularity for indoor use. Varieties with very large flowers in a range of pastel shades are sold, either in pots or as cut flowers. A member of the gentian family originating from Texas, it is somewhat cold-tender and the weak-stemmed flowers are easily damaged. Sow seed indoors in fall (autumn) or winter. Minimum temperature 40°F (4°C).

E. grandiflorum (syn. *Lisianthus russelianus*) to 18in (45cm), thin stems terminate in funnel-shaped blue, pink, or white flowers to 3in (7cm) across.

Exacum
ARABIAN VIOLET

Not a true violet but, like *Eustoma,* a member of the gentian family, this tiny shrublet charms by the profusion of its small, clear lavender-blue flowers, produced continuously for several months. Best treated as an annual and bought as a plant just as the first flowers open, or it can be raised from seed sown in fall (autumn). Minimum temperature 45°F (7°C).

E. affine compact rounded plant to

ABOVE: The petunia is easy to grow and makes a good display when massed together on a bench or table top.

10in (25cm) high, brittle fleshy stems; the numerous 1/2in (13mm) wide flowers are saucer-shaped.

Petunia

Possibly now the world's most popular summer bedding annual, petunias owe much to the extraordinary success of plant breeders. Apart from the amazing range of flower hues, shapes, and patterns, they are unmatched for their profusion of flowers over a long season and their indifference to hot weather that has other annuals drooping. Although usually planted outdoors, their virtues are so many that it is hard

not to include them in any selection of conservatory annuals. If a sunny position is available it should be possible to extend their season. Petunias like conditions that are not too soft, so do not water or fertilize them too much.

P. x *hybrida* includes all garden strains, height 10in (25cm) to 2ft (60cm) depending on the strain.

Primula

Relatives of the primrose and cowslip, most members of this large genus are hardy rock-garden and alpine plants but several are more tender and valued

ABOVE: Contrasting dark green foliage and soft pink flowers is the benefit of choosing plants such as fairy primrose (Primula malacoides).

for indoor use. With the exception of *P. malacoides* they are not strictly annuals but are generally treated as such. Primulas are unsuited to very warm conservatories and in summer may need to be removed outdoors to a cool sheltered position. They like good light and ample water. Minimum temperature 40°F (4°C).

P. malacoides (fairy primrose) fast-growing annual to 1ft (30cm), profuse small pink to purple flowers produced over a long season; free-seeding.

P. obconica clumps of broad basal leaves, showy clusters of 1in (2.5cm) wide flowers in a large range of pale to deep colours; to 1ft (30cm). Leaf contact causes allergic reaction in some people.

Salpiglossis
PAINTED TONGUE

Although never one of the more popular annuals, salpiglossis seldom fails to arouse comment and admiration for the beautiful feather-like markings of the trumpet-shaped flowers. These come in many hues, from cream through yellow and orange to violet, purple, pink, and red, with the markings generally a darker shade of the same basic hue. Sunshine is the main requirement, and the weak stems may need supporting. Sow seed in early spring for summer flowers. Minimum temperature 35°F (2°C).

S. sinuata is the sole species but includes a number of garden strains, mostly mixed hues. To 2ft (60cm), flowers to 2in (5cm) wide.

Schizanthus
POOR MAN'S ORCHID

These annuals are related to salpiglossis but have feathery leaves and smaller, more crowded flowers, the petals each deeply split into two lobes and with a richly marked upper lip, reminiscent of an orchid flower. Most seed strains include mixed hues, mainly pink, purple, yellow, and cream. Requirements are as for Salpiglossis.

S. pinnatus includes all the garden strains; to 15in (40cm) high, flowers about 1in (2.5cm) wide.

Senecio
CINERARIA

A traditional container plant and a feature in massed floral displays in public conservatories, cinerarias provide a wonderful show of flowers in a dazzling mixture of hues, but only over a fairly short season in early spring. They are suited only to cool conservatories, requiring a winter rest period before flowering. The easiest way to obtain a good display is to buy plants in bud in late winter; otherwise seed should be sown the previous

ABOVE: A bright display of flowers is guaranteed when you plant cinerarias
(Senecio cruenta) *as shown by the grouping in the photograph.*

summer. Cinerarias like good light, high humidity, and frequent watering, but dislike very high temperatures at any time. Minimum temperature 40°F (4°C).

S. x *hybridus* to 18in (45cm) high with densely massed, broad, toothed basal leaves topped by a broad head of daisy-like flowers; modern strains include white, blue, purple, pink, orange, and red flowers, often with a white inner ring.

Torenia

Useful and attractive little annuals from the tropics, torenias are valued for their unusual blue and purple pattern and for their extended flowering period which starts only weeks after sowing. As long as there is a reasonable level of light and adequate warmth they can be relied upon to bloom freely. Their compact size suits them to different situations in the conservatory, from massed plantings around the base of trees in tubs to hanging baskets or simply in the ground. Sow seed any time in spring or summer. Minimum temperature 40°F (4°C).

T. fournieri slender annual to 10in (25cm) high, stem with pairs of small soft leaves, flowers pale mauve-blue edged purple-brown, like a small pansy.

Tropaeolum
NASTURTIUM

Although quite hardy outdoors except in the most severe climates, nasturtiums are so well suited to planting in containers, especially in hanging baskets, and make such cheerful, easy-to-grow plants that it would seem a shame not to use them in the conservatory. Their one drawback, the lanky, bare older stems with untidy withering leaves, has been almost eliminated in some compact strains that have recently appeared. Nasturtiums prefer sun but will grow in reasonably bright reflected light. They are extraordinarily drought-tolerant and their flowering is discouraged by excessive watering and fertilizing. The young leaves can be used for eating in the same way as watercress and the unripe seedpods pickled like capers.

T. majus older forms mound to 18in (45cm) high and 3ft (1m) across, but newer strains are only about 1ft x 1ft (30cm x 30cm). Flowers range from cream through yellow, orange, and scarlet to deep brick red.

FLOWERING SHRUBS/PERENNIALS

Abutilon
CHINESE LANTERN, FLOWERING MAPLE

Grown as garden shrubs in warmer temperate regions, abutilons make long-lived conservatory plants which bear their pretty, pendent, bell-shaped flowers over a long season in summer and fall (autumn). Some have variegated leaves as well, usually an irregular mosaic of yellow or cream. Adapted to both cool and warm conservatories, they will survive winter temperatures of 50°F (10°C) or lower. Strong light, preferably some sunlight, is required for flowering.

A. x *hybridum* includes nearly all the tender evergreen varieties; shrubs to 8ft (2.4m) but can be trained to 2–3ft (60–90cm), leaves maple-like, flowers in a range of subdued shades from cream to deep maroon, up to 3in (7cm) diameter.

ABOVE: Position it in a sunny corner of the conservatory and the Abutilon x hybridum *'Golden fleece' will reward with an abundance of golden yellow flowers in summer. It can also be trained around a column.*

Anthurium
FLAMINGO FLOWER

With brilliant red, pink or green spoon-shaped "flowers", these anthuriums are among the most flamboyant of all the traditional hothouse plants. They are also surprisingly tough if certain basic requirements are met. Mostly epiphytes in the wild, they like to be potted in a container with perfect drainage but in a compost with good moisture retention, including, for example, chopped sphagnum moss. Keep in strong light but not sun, minimum temperature around 60°F (15°C).

A. *andraeanum* (painter's palette) is the larger of the two common species, with glossy "flowers" to 4in (10cm) wide, from brilliant red to white or pale green. Height to 2ft (60cm).

A. *scherzerianum* is the smaller and hardier species, with matt blooms in brilliant hues of red or pink to white, the central spike twisted. Height to 15in (40cm).

Begonia

A large group of plants, very diverse in foliage, bloom and growth-form. All have attractive flowers but many are grown primarily for their foliage. Even varieties with large brilliant flowers mostly have interesting foliage as well; the most frequently grown are the "cane" types, with stiff, upright or arching stems, narrow pointed leaves which are often spotted, and sprays of pink to orange or red flowers. Other classes are rhizomatous begonias with a short knotty rhizome on the soil surface; tuberous begonias which die back to a tuber annually; and fibrous-rooted begonias, which include the bedding begonias. A minimum temperature of 50°F (10°C) or higher is required. All types appreciate high humidity, but rhizomatous begonias should be watered sparingly, while tuberous

begonias are kept almost completely dry during their winter dormant period.

B. 'Orange Rubra' cane type to about 2ft (60cm) tall, bright orange flowers all year.

B. 'Lucerna' cane type to 6ft (1.8m), silver-spotted leaves, deep pink flowers all year.

B. masoniana (Iron Cross begonia) rhizomatous type to 12in (30cm), crinkled green leaves with chocolate "maltese cross" pattern, white flowers.

ABOVE: Always a favourite, Impatiens *is an easy to grow plant. This New Guinea hybrid* 'Lasting impressions' *has strong colour in both foliage and flower.*

Billbergia

Belonging to the Bromeliad (or pineapple) family, billbergias include some of the vase-shaped epiphytes unique to that group, as well as some with softer, more grassy foliage. The arching sprays of flowers have attractive soft-pink bracts. A few species are tough hardy plants tolerant of low temperatures and humidity, but the ones with richly marked foliage are more fussy, requiring a minimum of 55–60°F (13–15°C) and high humidity. A fibrous, open growing medium is preferred.

B. nutans the hardiest species, 12–15in (30–40cm), finely tapering leaves, many drooping flower-spikes, blue-striped flowers.

B. venezuelana 2ft (60cm), cylinder of wide leaves barred maroon and silver, drooping flower-spike with crowded pink bracts.

Columnea

These include some of the most dramatic plants for hanging baskets, their soft curtains of foliage dotted with bizarre orange to scarlet hooded flowers, adapted for pollination by tropical hummingbirds which hover beneath them to sip the nectar. Others are more spreading, scrambling plants. They thrive in heated conservatories with winter temperatures kept at 50–60°F (10–15°C) depending on species, in strong light but not sun.

C. gloriosa is the most spectacular, with masses of vertically hanging stems to 6ft (1.8m) long, large scarlet flowers.

Fittonia

Combining prettily marked leaves and curious spikes of small yellow flowers, fittonias have been used as conservatory plants since the mid 19th century. Ideally suited to hanging baskets, they like year round warmth and humidity and moderately high light. Minimum temperature 60°F (15°C).

F. verschaffeltii soft scrambling plant to 6in (15cm) high, oval bronze-green leaves with network of bright pink veins.

Hoya
WAX PLANT

Increasingly popular in recent years, hoyas are grown for their pretty clusters of waxy-textured white or pink (rarely darker red) flowers. The scrambling or twining stems and thick leathery leaves may appear coarse and untidy in some species, but this heightens the contrast with the neatness of the flowers. The climbing species are usually trained up wire frames or allowed to form a tangled ball of stems around a hanging basket, while the shrubby ones are grown in pots or baskets. Bright light (including sun) is essential. Avoid overwatering plants or overfeed or flowering will be poor. A winter rest period with very little watering is advised. Allow old flower heads to remain in place as they produce next year's flowers. Minimum temperature 50°F (10°C).

H. bella charming small shrub, trailing branches, small pointed leaves,

flat heads of starry white flowers with red in the middle.

H. carnosa is the best known, climbing to 8ft (2.4m) or more if allowed, globular clusters of pale pink flowers.

Impatiens
BUSY LIZZIE, BALSAM

The last decade or so has seen an explosion of new varieties of this plant. The newer forms flower continuously and profusely and come in a dazzling array of hues; one large group, derived from New Guinea species, has bronze or multi-hued leaves and includes brilliant oranges and scarlets in its range. Grow from cuttings or seed in summer. Cold tolerance varies, from frost-hardy (*I. balasamina*) to minimum 50°F (10°C) (New Guinea hybrids).

I. balsamina (garden balsams) shrubby annuals to 3ft (90cm), flowers mostly double in shades of white, rose, and salmon.

I. walleriana hybrids (impatiens, busy lizzie) varying height from 6in (15cm) to 2ft (60cm) or more, flowers all hues except yellow and orange, ever-blooming, often self-seeding, suit cool conservatory.

New Guinea hybrids mostly 15in (40cm) or less, spreading, leaves narrow and often patterned or bronzy, flowers large, white to deep scarlet.

Lotus
CORAL GEM

Consisting mostly of small pasture legumes, Lotus includes one species

from the Canary Islands with striking, large scarlet flowers, attracting birds which are its pollinators. With long trailing stems, it adapts well to hanging baskets and will flower freely if light level is high enough. Cool conservatory, minimum temperature 40°F (4°C).

L. berthelotii trailing stems to 3ft (1m) long with dense, fine silvery foliage, upturned beak-like scarlet flowers 2in (5cm) long in summer.

Plectranthus

Allied to *Coleus*, this is a large genus of mainly African soft shrubs and trailing plants, of which only a few have yet become popular for indoor growing. The main attraction is their fast growth and adaptability to a range of conditions, combined with pleasingly textured foliage; the small white to bluish flowers are not always produced. Best with minimum temperature of 50°F (10°C) though may survive much lower.

P. australis (Swedish ivy) trailing plant to 8in (20cm) high, crowded stems, small green leaves with scalloped edges (native to Africa, not Sweden!).

Portulaca
SUN PLANT

In addition to the varieties traditionally grown as summer bedding annuals, this group of succulents has given rise to newer strains, commonly sold for indoor use, with slightly smaller but

ABOVE: Delicate flowers and gorgeous colours are a feature of the Cape primrose (Streptocarpus).

neater flowers in shades of pink, orange, magenta, yellow, and cream, produced over a longer period. Available as container plants, they can be increased by cuttings. Overwinter at 50°F (10°C) or above.

P. grandiflora includes both bedding and indoor varieties, the latter distinguished by their flatter leaves and more prostrate stems; to 6in (15cm).

Saintpaulia
AFRICAN VIOLET

One of the most popular of indoor plants, the African violet is grown by many people who do not generally grow indoor plants. The kitchen or bathroom window ledge is its traditional location, though enthusiasts may set up elaborate growing stands for their African violets, complete with artificial light, automatic watering, or even hydroponics. The secrets of successful cultivation are high humidity in the immediate area, watering without wetting the leaves, minimum temperature of 55°F (13°C) or above, and reasonably high light level but not direct sun. Propagated from leaf cuttings.

S. ionantha is the main parent species, now represented by a vast array of hybrids with flowers from white to deepest purple, many of them double. Height from 2in (5cm) (miniatures) to 8in (20cm).

Streptocarpus
CAPE PRIMROSE

Relatives of African violets and gloxinias, these come in a range of growth forms from coarse rosettes with long-stemmed flowers to trailing plants suited to hanging baskets. Flowers feature a descending tube opening into an upturned "face", mostly in shades of purple. Requirements are similar to those of African violets, though some types are more tolerant of sun.

S. caulescens semi-trailing, to 8in (20cm) high, short hairy leaves, s mall pale violet flowers.

S. rexii hybrids are the type most commonly sold as container plants; height to 12in (30cm), they produce rosette of narrow leaves with a succession of flowering stems from the middle.

FOLIAGE PLANTS

Aspidistra
CAST-IRON PLANT

The indoor plant most familiar to earlier generations, the aspidistra is usually pictured as gathering dust in a dim corner of the room. But a well grown plant in the right container and the right setting is still one of the more elegant conservatory plants, with its classic long-stalked leaf shape. It will live just about for ever and its slow growth ensures that it will not get out of hand. Water sparingly, keep out of direct sun, and fertilize occasionally. Minimum temperature 45°F (7°C).
A. *elatior* is the common aspidistra, with dark green leaves springing from a buried rhizome to a height of about 2ft (60cm). The variety '**Variegata**' has random cream stripes in some of its leaves.

ABOVE: Richly patterned leaves and a variety of colours makes any of the Coleus blumei *species an attractive proposition for conservatories.*

Caladium
PAINTED LEAF

Leaves of caladiums are of the "elephant's ear" type and include some of the most beautifully hued and variegated leaves to be found among tropical foliage plants—carried on long stalks, they are marbled or veined white, green, pink or crimson and appear thin and delicate. Most caladiums are real hothouse plants, needing year-round warmth and humidity. They like strong light but not direct sun, and their tubers need a long dormant period in virtually dry soil.

Minimum temperature 65°F (18°C).
C. x *hortulanum* this hybrid includes numerous varieties, heights 1–3ft (30–90cm), leaves from white-veined green to solid scarlet-edged green.

Codiaeum
CROTON

Crotons are among the most popular shrubs in tropical gardens, prized for their brilliantly hued and interestingly shaped leaves. There are numerous named varieties. In colder climates they must be grown indoors, with winter minimum temperatures of 55–60°F (13–15°C). Long-lived and woody, they can grow to 5–8ft (1.5—2.4m) but as indoor plants are generally kept at 2–3ft (60–90cm). Bright light is required, preferably some sun, with plentiful watering in summer accompanied by frequent feeding with weak fertilizer solution.
C. *variegatum* is the only species. Popular varieties of it include '**Fascination**' (long leaves variably patterned green, red, and orange), '**Imperialis**' (yellow with pink edges, aging purple), '**Interruptum**' (long and narrow, twisted, yellow-edged green), and many others.

Coleus
COLEUS, PAINTED NETTLE

One of the "old fashioned" foliage plants, coleus was common on our grandparents' window ledges. The leaves are richly patterned in shades of pink, red, cream, purple, or chocolate, in many variations. So easy to propagate—just break off a soft branch tip in summer and "plant" it in a pot; in a warm place it will root in a few weeks. It is usual to renew plants annually in this way. Overwinter at 55°F (13°C) or higher.

C. blumei species includes many garden varieties, height to 2ft (60cm) or so; small bluish flowers are insignificant.

Dieffenbachia
DUMB CANE

Sometimes called "mother-in-law's tongue", possibly because the poison sap causes painful swelling of the tongue and loss of speech (but most unlikely to be tasted except by too-adventurous small children). Dieffenbachias are valued for their richly variegated large leaves and ability to survive indoors with minimal attention, though preferring humid conditions. When the plant gets too tall and lanky, just cut off the top and re-root in coarse compost. Minimum temperature 50°F (10°C).

D. picta is the common species, with many named forms, the large paddle-shaped leaves variously splashed or zoned cream to yellow. Grows to 3ft (1m).

Dracaena

Most dracaenas have narrow strap-leaves coming off a central "pole", but some have shorter and broader leaves from branched canes. One or two species are commonly sold as cut lengths of trunk sprouting from the top, under names such as "Chinese lucky plant". These will survive for a while just sitting in water, but should be properly potted for longer term survival. They require warmth, good drainage, and occasional feeding with weak nitrogenous fertilizer. Minimum temperature 50–55°F (10–13°C).

D. fragrans grows to 6ft (2m) or more with trunk to 3in (7.5cm) thick, crowded long floppy leaves striped yellow or cream.

D. godseffiana (gold-dust plant) 2–3ft (60–90cm) with many thin canes, the oval leaves densely yellow-spotted.

D. sanderiana weak leaning stems turning up at tips, to 2ft (60cm), thin tapering leaves with bold white stripes.

Epipremnum
DEVIL'S IVY

Ideal for warmer conservatories, devil's ivy is a lanky climber rather like the heart-leaved philodendron; if allowed to climb high enough on a wall or pole in good light its leaves get progressively larger, sometimes up to 1ft (30cm) across. Under good conditions its growth is quite fast, and it may need tying to its support. Both yellow and white variegated forms are grown. Minimum temperature 60°F (15°C).

E. aureum (syn. *Raphidophora aurea*, *Pothos aureus*) root climber to 10ft (3m) or more with broad, pointed glossy leaves variably splashed yellow.

Eucalyptus

Several species of this large group of Australian trees are grown under glass in cool climates for their ornamental foliage, maintained in the juvenile state by regular cutting back. Most attractive are those with rounded, waxy, bluish juvenile leaves. They are moderately cold-tolerant, surviving temperatures down to 30°F (–1°C), but must have good ventilation in hot humid weather. Grow in soil-based mix.

E. gunnii (Tasmanian cider gum) has pairs of bluish-silvery leaves encircling stiff twigs.

E. polyanthemos (silver dollar gum) has waxy, blue-silver, often pink-tinged, round drooping leaves tapering to stalk at base.

Ficus
ORNAMENTAL FIG, RUBBER PLANT

The weeping fig (*F. benjamina*) has become more popular than the rubber plant (*F. elastica*) during the last decade, especially since the upsurge of interest in trained and topiarised trees. Most figs do well as indoor plants, tolerating dry atmosphere and neglect of watering better than most. They are choosy about light levels though, shedding quantities of leaves if transferred to a spot where the light is too dim. Minimum temperature 45°F (7°C).

F. *benjamina* (weeping fig) 4–8ft (1.2–2.4m), fine drooping twigs, small shiny leaves.

F. *elastica* '**Schrijveriana**' (variegated rubber plant) 3–6ft (1–2m) single straight stem when young, large pointed leaves blotched cream and pale and dark green.

F. *lyrata* (fiddleleaf fig) 4–8ft (1.2–2.4m) stiff upright shrub, dull green leaves up to 12in (30cm) long, like a violin body in outline.

Hedera
IVY

Ivies in all their many varieties are so hardy outdoors that it may seem a waste of valuable heated space to grow them in a conservatory. But they do have the virtue of being among the easiest of all plants to look after as well as to propagate, and hence are ideal foliage plants for those indoor gardeners unwilling or unable to devote time to their plants. Ivies adapt to a variety of treatments, flowing over the rim of a tub or hanging basket, being trained up a pole, or clinging to a wall. Ivies like good light and frequent watering which wets the leaves, especially in warm conditions.

H. *canariensis* '**Variegata**' (Algerian ivy) is the common large-leaved variegated ivy, the leaves hardly lobed.

ABOVE: Long trails are the result of care and attention in the growing of ivy (Hedera). It is well worth the extra effort and heating bills.

H. helix (English ivy) comes in dozens of varieties, the leaves sharply lobed to rounded or with crisped edges, often variegated in many patterns.

Hypoestes
POLKA-DOT PLANT

A charming little tropical plant which makes fast growth, it gets its common name from the numerous round pink spots with which the small oval leaves are liberally scattered. A soft-wooded sub-shrub, it is suited to a pot or hanging basket in a brightly lit position. Water freely in summer, sparingly in winter. Minimum temperature 60°F (15°C).

H. phyllostachya weak sprawling stems to 15in (40cm), thin leaves spotted bright pink against a dull purple-green. '**Splash**' is a variety with larger blotches of pink merging with the dots.

Maranta
PRAYER PLANT

Among small, easily grown indoor plants the ground-hugging prayer plant is one of the most striking with the richly patterned variegation of its neat oval leaves. Against a dull green background is set a beautifully regular, feather-like pattern of long, fine red or white veins alternating with shorter blotches, while the leaf underside is wine-red or purple-silver. In the dark or in poor light the plant assumes a "sleeping position" with the leaves folded together (hence "prayer plant").

ABOVE: A familiar sight in many indoor plant schemes—the amusing freckle-face, polka dot plant (Hypoestes phyllostachya).

Grow in a shallow pot or hanging basket away from strong light, water often in summer.

M. leuconeura only about 4in (10cm) high but spreading widely, leaves pale green with chocolate markings along mid rib. '**Erythroneura**' is a variety with bright red veins and very pale green blotches a against deep green background.

Peperomia

Peperomias are ideal foliage plants for the smaller conservatory, as their growth is very compact. A diverse collection of species can readily be acquired, the mainly green leaves exhibiting a tremendous variety of sizes, shapes and textures. The long "rat-tail" spikes of minute flowers are an interesting feature. Cultivation is fairly simple, the main requirement being repotting every two years or so in fresh, very coarse compost. Keep in good light but not direct sun, water sparingly, and trim away old leaves. Minimum temperature 55°F (13°C).

P. caperata dense cluster to 8in (20cm) high of long-stalked, round leaves with deeply wrinkled surfaces. '**Emerald Ripples**' is a more compact form.

P. argyreia (watermelon plant) 8in

(20cm) high, fleshy, concave round
leaves with converging broad silver
stripes.

P. magnoliifolia 'Variegata' more
robust plant to 1ft (30cm) with fleshy
stems, smooth paddle-shaped leaves
blotched yellow.

Philodendron

Another very traditional indoor plant,
the common heart-leaved philodendron will happily climb up walls,
around doorways and windows, and
even onto the ceiling if given free rein.
But
philodendrons include a much wider
range of growth-forms and leaf-shapes,
from dense rosettes to massive shrubs,
as well as climbers. Many are
remarkably tough, coping with dry
atmosphere, strong sun or dim corners,
or infrequent watering; a few thinner-
leaved species are more delicate.
All are long-lived. Minimum
temperature 50°F (10°C).

P. cordatum (heart-leaved philodendron) climber to 8ft (2.4m) or more,
green heart-shaped leaves.

P. pedatum semi-climbing, compact
growth to 6ft (1.8m), large green
leaves with about five curved lobes.

P. selloum grows to a large shrub 8ft
(2.4m) high and at least as wide,
the giant leaves divided into many
narrow lobes.

P. 'Burgundy' robust climber to
6ft (1.8m), large glossy arrowhead-
shaped leaves are wine-red on
underside.

Sansevieria
SNAKE PLANT, MOTHER-
IN-LAW'S TONGUE

The sansevieria is often viewed in
the same light as the aspidistra—like
an item of furniture which sits for
years in a corner of the room and
receives the minimum of attention. If
anything, the sansevieria is even more
tolerant of this treatment, clinging to
life with great tenacity, but like most
such plants it responds gratefully to
kinder treatment. In the conservatory
it can look great massed in a large tub.
Requires warm growing season and
minimum temperature of 55°F
(13°C)in winter.

S. trifasciata with succulent sword-
shaped leaves to 18in (45cm) tall,
includes most of the popular varieties:
notably '**Laurentii**', leaves cross-band-
ed dark green, edges yellow; '**Hahnii**',
leaves very short forming a rosette,
broad yellow edges; '**Moonshine**',
leaves to 1ft (30cm), pale silvery-green
with fine dark green edge.

Schefflera
UMBRELLA TREE

Some indoor foliage plants are merely
the younger stages of quite large trees,
as seen outdoors in the tropics. The
young umbrella tree has a single thick
stem bearing large compound leaves,
the stalks of the large oblong leaflets
radiating from a central leafstalk like
the spokes of an umbrella. The bold
pattern of its fresh green foliage suits it
for use in interior design, much like a
potted palm. Good light, frequent
watering in summer, and applications
of weak soluble fertilizer will ensure
success. Minimum temperature 60°F
(15°C).

S. actinophylla (Queensland umbrella
tree) vertical stem 3–8ft (1–2.4m)
high, ultimately a tree, leaflets up to
12in (30cm) long.

S. arboricola (miniature umbrella tree)
3–6ft (1–2m) with spreading branches,
the crowded leaflets only 4in (10cm)
or so long.

Tradescantia
WANDERING JEW

Grown chiefly for their foliage, trades-
cantias fall into the "impossible to kill"
class of indoor plants—though like
most such plants they will always look
far better when treated with a little
tender loving care. The thin trailing
stems root at the joints and the oval
leaves are green to purplish and often
striped. They survive winter temperatures of 40°F (4°C) or even less but
maintain growth best at 60°F (15°C).
Plants previously classified as *Setcreasea*
and *Zebrina* are now included in
Tradescantia.

T. albiflora one of the toughest, with
trailing stems, leaves to 3in (7cm)
long, plain green or striped white,
sometimes also purple, or blotched
yellow.

T. purpurea (syn. *Setcreasea purpurea*)
has shorter, more upright stems to 12in
(30cm) high; long channeled leaves are
deep purple on both sides.

ABOVE: Ornamental chilies (capsicum) grow well in the correct conditions in a conservatory and are attractive as display plants.

EDIBLE PLANTS

Ananas comosus
PINEAPPLE

Easily grownin a heated conservatory. Plants are readily obtained by planting the cut-off leafy tops from pineapples, and will bear fruit in two to three years. Provide as much sun and water as possible and fertilize with a 10:6:10 liquid fertilizer applied to the leaves, or fruits will be very small and sour. Minimum temperature 55°F (13°C). A variegated form is very ornamental.

Arachis hypogaea
PEANUT

Easily grown in any good loose-textured soil, a peanut plant makes an interesting talking point in the conservatory. Buy fresh raw peanuts and plant just like bean seeds, though deeper— 3in (8cm). Germination requires soil temperature of 65°F (13°C) or higher. Small yellow flowers appear among crowded stems, developing pods push beneath the soil.

Capsicum spp.
CHILIES

Easily grown all year in a warm conservatory, or in summer in a cool conservatory. The fruit comes in many shapes, sizes, and hues, its hotness being in inverse proportion to size. Annual types should be sown about two months in advance, while the shrubby ones will live many years if winter temperatures are above 32°F (0°C).

C. annuum annuals to 2ft (60cm), includes all the medium and larger fruited chilies and peppers, also some small but elongated ones.

C. frutescens softwooded shrub to 5ft (1.5m), leaves small, fruit globular to bullet-shaped, less than 3/4in (2cm) long.

Cichorium endivia, C. intybus
ENDIVE, CHICORY

Fashionable these days as leaf vegetables and resembling some varieties of lettuce, endive and chicory are best suited to the cool conservatory. The blanched hearts, known as chicons and witloof, are usually grown in cellars. The green and red leafy types are treated in much the same way as lettuce.

Above: There is great pleasure to be had in picking one's own citrus fruit in the conservatory for breakfast. Shown here are the fruit of a Citrus paradisi.

Citrus and Fortunella spp.
CITRUS FRUITS

The culture of citrus fruits in conservatories goes back centuries in Europe. Oranges, grapefruit, tangerines, and citrons all adapt well to the cool conservatory while lemons and limes prefer a winter minimum of around 50°F (10°C). Grown in tubs they can be kept to a height of 3–6ft (1–2m) and make attractive ornamentals.

Citrus aurantifolia (Lime) green thin-skinned fruit has a distinctive acid taste.

Citrus aurantium (Seville orange) branches bears spines, fruit used for marmalade.

Citrus limon (Lemon) irregular open shrub, large leaves. The variety '**Meyer**' is most cold-tolerant.

Citrus mitis (Calamondin) curious shrub with small crowded leaves, ornamental but sour orange fruit.

Citrus paradisi (Grapefruit) broad rounded shrub with dense foliage.

Citrus reticulata (Tangerine) upright habit, small leaves, bears well in cooler conditions.

Citrus sinensis (Sweet orange) broad rounded shrub, includes several well-known varieties including '**Jaffa**', '**Navel**', '**Ruby**' (blood orange), '**Valencia**'.

Fortunella japonica (Cumquat) bears abundant small but sour fruit when only 2ft (60cm) high.

Coffea arabica
COFFEE

Normally an upright shrub of about 8ft (2.5m), a coffee plant can be kept smaller by restricting its roots in a tub or large pot. Surprisingly hardy, it will tolerate winter temperatures of 50°F (10°C), but needs a long growing season at 70°F (21°C) or higher. Pretty white flowers line the branches in spring followed by dull red berries in summer. Expect to harvest only a token amount of beans from your plant.

Coriandrum sativum
CORIANDER

A summer-growing herb, valued now mainly for its pungent-tasting leaves which provide one of the most important taste ingredients in many Asian cuisines. The ripe seeds are also used in curries and seasonings. A heated conservatory can provide year-round supplies of the fresh leaves, which can be picked only a few weeks after sowing, and even a cool conservatory will extend the growing season.

Cucumis sativus
CUCUMBER

This subtropical vegetable is traditionally grown under glass in colder climates. The vines are trained on to parallel wires strung at 6in (15cm) intervals just below the glass. Germination and seedling growth require a temperature of 65°F (18°C) while fruit production is optimum at 70°F (21°C). Plant in friable well-manured soil in pots or trays and water well. Ventilation is necessary in hot weather.

ABOVE: These interesting-looking fruit are none other than fleshy figs on the branch. The Ficus carica *likes the atmosphere of a cool conservatory.*

Ficus carica
FIG

A fig tree will grow and bear figs in the cool conservatory and can be kept to a compact size by confining the roots (which also promotes fruiting) and by pruning when leafless. Too much water and humidity in summer results in mildew on leaves and fruit. Full sun, minimum temperature 30°F (−1°C).
'**Brown Turkey**' is a variety suited to indoor planting.

Fragaria x ananassae
STRAWBERRY

The traditional strawberry pot, with several apertures below the rim, is one of the best and most attractive ways of growing this delicious fruit indoors. Strawberries can be grown in either cool or warm conservatories and year-round cropping is possible in the warm ones. Strawberries should be replanted annually from runners for best results.

Lactuca sativa
LETTUCE

This salad green is perhaps the easiest of all vegetables to grow under glass. If garden space is available it is better grown outdoors when frosts are past. Artificial heat is not required except in very cold climates. Non-hearted types such as cos, mignonette, and butterhead are best for conservatories, taking only a few weeks from planting out to harvesting. A variety of leaf shades and forms are available and can make a decorative display if combined in shallow pots or trays.

Lycopersicon esculentum
TOMATO

From cherry-size to apple-size, deep red to pale yellow, round to oval, tomatoes come in many sizes, shapes and hues. They can make a quite decorative element in the conservatory as well as its most valued crop. The dwarf, smaller-fruited varieties are the best for indoors and some will crop continuously over several months. Heat is needed for spring cropping; seedlings need a temperature of 60°F (15°C) or higher for satisfactory growth. In hot summer weather, plants should be moved outdoors.

Ocimum basilicum
BASIL

No lover of good food these days is content without fresh basil leaves, an essential ingredient for many salads and for pesto sauce. A heated conservatory should provide year-round supplies, if new plants are started about every six weeks. One or two flourishing plants should supply the average household. Discard as soon as flowers are well advanced. Ample sun and water are the chief requirements.

Origanum vulgare
OREGANO

Also known as wild marjoram, oregano is among the most highly regarded of all cooking herbs in Mediterranean countries such as France, Italy, and Greece. It contributes a distinctive taste to Bolognese sauce eaten with pasta. A sprawling perennial, easily grown in a pot, it develops its best taste under warm sunny conditions. Leaves and flower buds are harvested and used fresh or dried. For the cool conservatory; will survive winter frost.

Petroselinum crispum
PARSLEY

One of the most popular culinary and salad herbs and the main ingredient of Lebanese tabbouleh, parsley is readily grown in pots in the cool conservatory. Start from seed or buy seedlings in late winter or spring; harvest the leaves through summer, fall (autumn), and into winter. Once the flowering stems are fully elongated the plants should be discarded.

Vitis vinifera and hybrids
GRAPE

Grape vines are greedy for space and normally are only grown in conservatories if the climate is too cold for outdoor cropping. In northern Europe they have been grown under glass since the 16th century or earlier. In most circumstances artificial heat is undesirable. In summer and early fall

ABOVE: The cherry tomato (Lycopersicon esculentum) *plant is rich red and delicious as well. See listing on previous page.*

(autumn) when the fruit is ripening, humidity must be kept low by adequate ventilation, or the vines will become mildewed. Table grape varieties give fewer problems than some of the famous wine grapes.

Zea mays
SWEET CORN

Compact varieties of sweet corn grow to only 3–5ft (1m–1.5m) high and are suitable for the conservatory. Perhaps it is something of a luxury to grow such a low-priced vegetable in a heated conservatory, but it certainly provides a mass of fresh green foliage. Seedling growth requires a temperature of 60–64°F (16–18°C) or more, and the cool conservatory can be used to start plants in spring for early summer harvesting. Ornamental forms are also available with variegated leaves or multi-hued cobs.

Zingiber officinale
GINGER

A strictly tropical spice plant, ginger needs a heated conservatory even to survive the colder winters. Obtaining a plant is easy—just buy a large, healthy piece of fresh ginger and place it on top of moist potting mix in a medium-size pot. The elegant leafy shoots grow to about 2ft (60cm) high. It is chiefly of curiosity value, unless you cannot buy fresh ginger. Minimum temperature 50°F (10°C).

FERNS AND THEIR ALLIES

Adiantum
MAIDENHAIR FERN

Maidenhairs are among the most delicately beautiful of all ferns, with frothy masses of small, rounded fresh green leaflets on fine wiry stalks. As houseplants they are traditionally perceived as suited to the bathroom or kitchen, reflecting their need for high humidity and protection from sun. In a conservatory they like to be positioned beside a pool or cascade if these features are present; otherwise against a shaded wall. In warm weather frequent mist-spraying is advisable, but avoid overwatering the soil. Minimum temperature 50°F (10°C).

A. raddianum is the commonly planted species, with numerous named varieties. To 18in (45cm) high, massed fronds, also spilling down. Varieties differ in size and lobing of leaflets; some are lime-green or golden green.

Asplenium
SPLEENWORT

The spleenworts are an interesting group of ferns, mostly with rather leathery fronds in a wide range of shapes and sizes. They include the birds-nest ferns, large epiphytes with rosettes of broad fronds, as well as many other species with finely divided fronds; some of these are noteworthy for the small plantlets that develop on the fronds, giving rise to names such as

ABOVE: One of the most beautiful and popular ferns is the maidenhair fern (Adiantum raddianum) with its massed fronds creating a spectacular focal point.

"hen-and-chicken fern". These ferns are easily grown in cool as well as warm conservatories, tolerating winter temperatures down to 40°F (4°C) or lower. Water frequently in summer.

A. bulbiferum (hen-and-chicken fern) has arching plume-like fronds to 18in (45cm) high, with few to many bulbous-based plantlets which can be detached and rooted.

A. nidus (birds-nest fern) makes a rosette of paddle-shaped flattish fronds up to 3ft (90cm) long and 6in (15cm) wide.

Cyrtomium
HOLLY FERN

A tough, easily grown fern which at the same time is very ornamental. It has broad, coarsely toothed leaflets which are glossy green on the upper side but are covered beneath in silvery scales, as well as being (at maturity) densely spotted with red-brown sporecases. In size and outline the leaflets are reminiscent of holly leaves. This fern needs good light and humidity in hot weather but avoid watering it excessively. Minimum temperature 50°F (10°C).

C. falcatum has stiffly spreading fronds from a central root mass, up to 15in (40cm) high.

Doryopteris
HAND FERN

A small tropical fern with very neat attractive fronds which are curiously divided in a somewhat hand-like form.

Cultivation can be tricky, as the plant resents too much humidity or soil that stays damp. Light level should be high without direct sun, and warmth and ventilation adequate during the growing season. Minimum temperature 55°F (13°C).

D. pedata forms a small tight clump about 8in (20cm) high, the deeply lobed fronds carried on wiry black stalks.

Nephrolepis
FISHBONE FERN

Apart from maidenhairs, this group of decorative ferns is the most widely sold. The basic plan of the ferns' elongated fronds is well conveyed by the name "fishbone" but intensive selection of mutations has produced numerous variants, mostly more finely dissected to varying degrees. Cultivation is not too difficult, and large and beautiful specimens can be produced in hanging baskets or in shallow tubs. Light should be bright but without direct sun. Frequent watering and, preferably, mist-spraying is necessary in warm weather. Minimum temperature 50°F (10°C).

N. cordifolia is the hardier species and spreads by long stringy rhizomes bearing hard bulbils. '**Plumosa**' is an attractive form with ends of leaflets finely lobed and plume-like, fronds semi-pendulous.

N. exaltata (Boston fern) is represented mainly by its named varieties of which there are many, most being suited to hanging baskets.

'**Suzie Wong**' is a recent variety with extremely finely divided, frothy foliage.

Platycerium
STAGHORN FERN

A fully grown staghorn fern could be the *pièce de résistance* of your conservatory. These massive epiphytes consist of a "nest" of upright, broadly sheathing fronds and one or more large, pendulous, repeatedly forked spore-bearing fronds. A large plant can be as much as 10ft (3m) from top to bottom, but even at half that size they have a dramatic impact. Successful cultivation requires the plant to be initially tied to a vertical surface, for example a large slab of weathered hardwood, or the outside of a fiber-packed basket. The fern must have strong light and will take full sun if hardened off first. Avoid overwatering; mist-spray in hot weather. Feed from the top with weak liquid manure. Minimum temperature 55°F (13°C).

P. superbum is one of the largest and handsomest species, its pendulous frond up to 6ft (1.8m) long and as much across; its paler upright "nest" fronds are also very large and many-lobed.

Polystichum
SHIELD FERN

This is a group of ground ferns with dense, finely divided fronds and very scaly rhizomes; most of the species are relatively cold-hardy and will do well in a cool conservatory. Cultivation is straightforward, the plants' chief requirements being moderately bright light but not direct sun, frequent watering, and reasonably constant warmth during the growing season. If temperature is low in winter the plants may become dormant. Minimum temperature 30–50°F (–1–10°C) depending on the species.

P. tsus-simense has a compact habit, to 12in (30cm) tall, the small leaflets in many neat rows.

Pteris
BRAKE FERN

A large worldwide genus of ferns which includes both tropical and cold-hardy species. Most are ground ferns with long-stalked fronds, roughly triangular in outline but usually divided into linear segments. Some of the most popular forms are variegated or double hued variants of certain species. They are generally vigorous growers requiring medium to high light levels and frequent watering. Minimum temperature 55°F (13°C) for the species.

P. cretica 'Albolineata' (Cretan brake) a very popular fern to 15in (40cm) tall, three to nine long narrow leaflets each with a central zone of creamy green.

RIGHT: The silver brake fern (Pteris argyraea) *with a narrow leaf is to the left at the back of this photograph;* Pteris argyraea *cv.* Victoriae *is to the fore.*

P. argyraea (silver brake) forms a clump up to 3ft (1m) tall. The large frond is divided into broad, deeply lobed segments, each with a broad silver central stripe.

Selaginella
CLUBMOSS

Not true ferns, selaginellas seem halfway between ferns and mosses in appearance. In moist shaded soil they will spread widely, the fronds springing from slender rhizomes. Some species are remarkably easy to grow, needing only plentiful water and a modest amount of light, and may even behave as weeds in the containers of other plants. Others are more demanding, in that they require sustained warmth and humidity to make their growth; all are shade-lovers. Minimum temperature 40–55°F (4–13°C) depending on the species.

S. kraussiana a carpeting plant for moist soil; or makes an attractive green ball in a hanging basket. '**Aurea**' is a golden form, less vigorous.

S. willdenovii (electric fern) has long scrambling stems with regular fans of foliage of a remarkable iridescent blue. To 3ft (1m) high, requires warmth and high humidity.

RIGHT: Its slow growth, elegant shape and dark green shiny leaves make the kentia palm (Howea forsterana) a popular indoor and conservatory plant.

PALMS AND PALM-LIKE PLANTS

Beaucarnea
PONYTAIL PALM

Not a true palm but a relative of the yuccas and agaves. This slightly bizarre but quite elegant plant gets along for years with minimal attention, but only if it is in sufficiently strong light, preferably some direct sun. Small plants start out with a golfball-size, brown bulbous stem topped by a "ponytail" of long, finely tapering, recurving leaves. The "bulb" builds up in size with age (in very old plants up to 8ft (2.4m) across at the base!) and at the same time develops a tapering stem above. Grow in a pot, then a tub, and finally in the ground if your conservatory is big enough. Minimum temperature 35°F (2°C).

B. recurvata is the species usually grown, height to 3ft (1m)in a pot or 8ft (2.4m)in the ground, channeled leaves 3–6ft (1–2m) long; trunk forks with age.

Caryota
FISHTAIL PALM

Unique among palms for their bipinnate (twice-divided) fronds with fishtail-shaped leaflets, caryotas can make outstandingly beautiful conservatory plants when young and vigorous, but their delicate green foliage can quickly become scorched and tattered if conditions are not ideal.

They need warmth and humidity, high light levels but protected from direct sun, and ample water all year but especially in summer. Apply weak soluble fertilizer (high nitrogen) at regular intervals. Minimum temperature 55°F (13°C).

C. mitis (clustered fishtail palm) has clustered shoots, the erect fronds to 6–8ft (1.8–2.4m) high in a pot or tub, new leaflets lime-green.

Chamaedorea
BAMBOO PALM

This large group of rainforest undergrowth palms from Mexico and Central America includes many of the most popular palms for indoor use, valued for their ease of cultivation as well as their elegant forms. The smooth bamboo-like stems are only pencil-thick in some species, up to 2in (5cm) thick in others, and may be solitary or form dense or open clumps. The leaves vary from pinnately divided to undivided with a two-lobed tip. Flower-spikes on some species are bright orange or yellow, contrasting with fruits. Good light but not direct sun is preferred, and plentiful water. Minimum temperature 50°F (10°C).

C. elegans (parlour palm) single stem to 4ft (1.2m) high, 1/2in (13mm) diameter, compact crown of short feathery leaves.

C. metallica single thin stem to 3ft (1 m), small tuft of narrow, undivided silvery leaves with metallic sheen.

C. erumpens (bamboo palm) clump of thin bamboo-like stems to 7ft (2m), with scattered short leaves each with four to ten leaflets

Chrysalidocarpus
GOLDEN CANE PALM

When fully grown this very elegant palm from Madagascar is too large for any but the largest conservatories. It forms a clump of stems diverging from ground-level; with age, each stem can extend into a trunk up to 8ft (2.4m) long, but trunks are unlikely to develop in a pot or tub. It is the long leafstalks that appear like yellowish "canes"; these bear many long narrow leaflets towards their ends. Warm growing conditions and strong light are required for success with this palm. Minimum temperature 55°F (13°C).

C. lutescens is the only commonly grown species, with erect fronds rising to a height of about 6ft (1.8m).

Cordyline

Another group of palm-like plants which are not really palms, cordylines have trunks which thicken and fork with age, topped by tufts of sword-like or paddle-like leaves. Many varieties have been developed with brightly hued foliage and these are very popular in tropical landscaping. Ease of propagation is a feature of cordylines, the cut-off tops or even short sections of trunk quickly rooting and sprouting. They need strong light and plentiful water in summer. Minimum winter temperature depends on the species.

C. australis (New Zealand cabbage tree) has stiff upright leaves only half an inch (1cm) wide in the juvenile state, increasing to 1in (2.5cm) or more with age. Height is 3–6ft (1–2m)in a pot. A form with purplish foliage is grown. Minimum temperature 30°F (–1°C).

C. terminalis (ti plant) has leaves to 4in (10cm) broad, narrowing to a rolled stalk. Its varieties have leaves from yellow-green through pink to bronze, red, or deep purple, often in stripes; some are "miniatures" with much smaller leaves. Height 2–6ft (0.6–2m). Minimum temperature 55°F (13°C).

Howea
KENTIA PALM

For 100 years or more this has been *the* potted palm, grown in conservatories, lobbies, ballrooms, and other indoor spaces throughout the world's temperate zones. In nature it is confined to tiny Lord Howe Island in the Tasman Sea between Australia and New Zealand. Two species grow together there. In mild climates the kentia grows to around 30ft (9m) outdoors. As an indoor plant it is usually discarded after it reaches 8ft or so— but this can take up to 30 years! Slow growth, combined with elegant shape and tolerance of poor conditions, account for its eternal popularity. Good light (not direct sun) is necessary for long-term health, though kentias will survive darker

corners for months on end. Minimum temperature 50°F (10°C).

H. forsterana has dark green leathery fronds up to 8ft (2.4m) long, with arching narrow leaflets and long basal stalk.

Phoenix
DATE PALM

About a dozen species from Asia and Africa make up the date palm genus, *Phoenix,* but only one is suited well to indoor use. Tough, durable palms, they are easily identifiable by the way the lower leaflets of each frond are transformed into rigid, sharp-pointed spines. Strong light, even direct sun, is desirable for good growth. Avoid watering too heavily. Minimum temperature 50°F (10°C).

P. roebelenii (miniature date palm) grows to about 6ft (1.8m) with rough-textured trunk and compact crown of elegant, finely feathery, recurving fronds.

Reinhardtia
WINDOW PALM

One of the choicer small palms to become widely available during the last decade, the window palm is so named for the row of small apertures or "windows" in its curiously shaped small leaflets. It is a delicate cluster-stemmed palm with stems hardly more than pencil-thick. A mature specimen can flower and fruit for several years in a medium-size pot; coral-red fruiting

branches liven its appearance. Requires warmth, humidity, ample water, medium light level. Minimum temperature 55°F (13°C).

R. gracilis has several stems 18in–3ft (45 90cm) high, fronds only 8in (20cm) consisting of four toothed leaflets.

Rhapis
LADY PALM

Attractive small clumping palms with glossy pleated leaf segments, lady palms have been prized as pot plants in Japan for centuries. More recently in Japan a collecting cult has arisen concentrating on dwarf and variegated mutations of *Rhapis,* the most sought after of which fetch extremely high prices for a single shoot. These aside, the ordinary lady palm makes a beautiful conservatory specimen and can be kept indefinitely in a large tub. High temperatures are not necessary but the plants appreciate humidity or frequent foliage misting. They should be sheltered from direct sun. Minimum temperature 40°F (5°C).

R. excelsa has blackish fibrous stems to 7ft (2m) high and 1in (2.5cm) in diameter. The scattered leaves each have five to ten radiating segments.

OPPOSITE: The cute shape of a peanut cactus (Chamaecereus silvestrii) makes it essential in any cactus collection.

CACTI AND SUCCULENTS

Aloe

Small to large succulents from Africa, aloes have rosettes of fleshy tapering leaves, sometimes spotted and often with spiny teeth on their edges. Tubular red or yellowish flowers are crowded on a central spike. They make tough indoor plants which are hard to kill. In the cool conservatory they should be watered sparingly in winter. Minimum temperature 40°F (4°C).

A. aristata small plant, crowded soft leaves with bristly tips and teeth.

A. saponaria to about 2ft (60cm), broad fleshy leaves spotted whitish.

A. vera narrow rosette of channeled, silvery green fleshy leaves to 15in (40cm). The pulped leaves and extracted sap have cosmetic and healing properties.

Cephalocereus
OLD MAN CACTUS

One of the most bizarre cacti but at the same time rather beautiful, old man cactus appears like a short pole completely covered in long, tangled white hairs, almost like human hair. Small plants are commonly sold and will survive and grow indoors for many years if their basic requirements of strong light, good ventilation, free-draining soil mix, and infrequent watering are met. Minimum temperature 40°F (5°C).

C. senilis grows with age to 2ft (60cm) or more and 2in (5cm) thick.

ABOVE: Eye-catching it may be but watch out for the ferocious yellow spines of this beauty, golden ball cactus (Echinocactus grusonii).

Chamaecereus
PEANUT CACTUS

One of the cutest cacti, with crowded, soft-spined, sprawling stems which produce quite unexpectedly large brilliant scarlet flowers in spring and summer. Seen at its best in a hanging pot or basket with stems spilling over the edge. Likes rich but free-draining soil mix and summer watering, but very little water in winter. Minimum temperature 40°F (5°C).

C. silvestrii stems 1/2in (12mm) in diameter, up to 1ft (30cm) long with age; flowers 2 1/2in (6cm) across.

Echinocactus
GOLDEN BALL CACTUS

Although a large genus of cacti, *Echinocactus* is best known by this one eye-catching species, frequently displayed in major cactus collections. Apart from the ferocious attraction of its dense golden yellow spines, its appeal lies in its ability to keep increasing in size almost indefinitely. Its chief requirement is bright sunlight, good ventilation, and a winter rest period at temperatures of 40–50°F (4–10°C) with soil virtually dry. In spring and summer, frequent watering and judicious fertilizing will make for maximum growth.

E. grusonii ultimately grows to about 3ft (1m) high and 2 1/2ft (75cm) in diameter, with many narrow vertical ribs and strong yellow spines. Globular plants about 8in (20cm) in diameter are often available.

Epiphyllum
LEAF CACTUS

A large group of epiphytic cacti in which the leafless stems are thin and flattened, or sometimes three- or four-winged; grown mostly for their large brilliant flowers. The majority of epiphyllums available are hybrids, often known by the collective names 'phyllocactus' or 'epicactus'. They require warmth and humidity and are ideally suited to being grown in hanging baskets. In spring and summer, water freely until flowering finishes; then allow a one month rest period with the soil barely moist. Medium light levels suit epiphyllums best. Minimum temperature 45°F (7°C).

E. oxypetalum a night-flowering species with white blooms 6in (15cm) across, tapering below into a long tube. Stems grow in all directions, to 3ft (1m).

E. 'Ackermannii' a very old hybrid but still popular, to 18in (45cm), flowers bright red, 4in (10cm) across, very profuse.

E. 'Sweet Alibi' modern hybrid, height 18in (45cm), flowers soft rose, 6in (15cm) across.

Kalanchoe

Consisting of many succulent species from Africa and Madagascar, *Kalanchoe* is best known as an indoor plant in the form of one profusely flowering species which has given rise to many improved varieties. These are sold in full bloom and commonly discarded when flowering has finished, but it is quite possible to keep them growing for at least another season or to take cuttings and thereby perpetuate the plants. Kalanchoes appreciate bright light, even direct sun, but should be watered sparingly and rested in winter with soil barely moist. Minimum temperature 50°F (10°C).

K. blossfeldiana has both large and small-growing forms, height 6–18in (15–45cm). Leaves flat, fleshy, rounded. Flowers red, pink, cream, yellow or orange, in dense heads.

Lithops
LIVING STONES

From the temperate deserts of far south-western Africa come these most amazing small succulents, bizarre representatives of the large mesembryanthemum family. When planted among rounded pebbles it is truly difficult to tell the plants from the stones. In a range of subdued silvery hues, greens,

ABOVE: The orange in this example of the succulent species Kalanchoe blossfeldiana *from Africa and Madagascar is most attractive.*

ABOVE: Looking a bit like a rolled up mohair pullover is this example of Mammillaria bocasana.

pinks and browns and often mottled or wrinkled, they are designed for camouflage. Yellow flowers, often larger than the plant itself, burst from between the two fused leaves that form the plant body. Grow in strong light but not direct sun; support plant in a layer of coarse gravel or pebbles so only the roots contact the soil. Water weekly from spring to fall (autumn), no water at all in winter. Minimum temperature 45°F (7°C).

L. lesliei is just one of many similar species; cylindrical to 1in (2.5cm) wide with flattened top, dull pinkish brown, mottled green.

Mammillaria

One of the largest groups of true cacti, consisting entirely of very compact plants but showing a tremendous variety of shape, hue, spine formation and features such as hairs and "wool", not to mention flowers. These miniature cacti have clusters of small finger-like stems, easily broken off, others form mounds of little balls, while there are many with solitary stems, either ball-shaped or short columns. Cultivation varies from very easy to extremely difficult depending on the species, but the ones widely sold are all easy. Their chief requirements are good light, no overwatering and a winter rest period with virtually no water. Minimum temperature 45°F (7°C).

M. bocasana (powder-puff cactus) cluster of balls almost concealed in long silky hairs, rings of small cream flowers followed by deep red fruits.

M. elongata cluster of finger-like stems to 6in (15cm) long, masked by radiating yellow, white, or reddish spines.

M. longimamma mound of flattened balls, each divided into plump green nipples tipped by yellow spines; small yellow flowers.

Schlumbergera
CHRISTMAS CACTUS,
CLAW CACTUS

These ever popular cacti give a profuse display of shapely pink flowers from the tips of its leaf-like stems over the northern hemisphere Christmas period. In recent years the original species has given way to a range of hybrids in different hues and shades. The plants are often discarded after flowering but with a little attention can be maintained for many years. Their arching-over habit makes schlumbergeras suited to hanging b askets, and their roots appreciate the aeration these containers provide. Place in good light but not direct sun; keep away from artificial light after buds form or the flowers will abort. Water frequently in the growing season. Minimum temperature 40°F (4°C).

S. truncata to 10in (25cm) high with arching branches, pendulous orchid-pink flowers.

S. '**Christmas Cheer**' is a hybrid with orange-red petals, cream stamens.

ABOVE: Less cuddly in appearance, but still an interesting plant, is this Mammillaria longimamma.

BULBS

Clivia
KAFFIR LILY

An evergreen bulb that is not truly a bulb but is usually classed as such because of its habit of growth and lily-like flowers. The flowers are carried in dense heads above deep green, broad strap-like leaves and are bright scarlet-orange grading to soft yellow in the throat. Masses of thick roots will eventually cram the pot, but the plant thrives in this state and need not be repotted in a hurry—just water freely (except in winter) and apply weak soluble fertilizer at intervals. Best suited to the cool conservatory as it requires a cool rest period in winter. Minimum temperature 40°F (4°C).

C. miniata has crowded, dark green recurving leaves about 2ft (60cm) long and 2in (5cm) wide; the flowering stalk is 18in (45cm) high.

ABOVE: A burst of colour among the glossy leaves of a kaffir lily (Clivia miniata).

Cyclamen

Though related to primulas, cyclamens are generally classified as bulbs by gardeners. The many smaller species are hardy rock-garden plants but the larger *C. persicum*, with numerous varieties, is a traditional conservatory plant. These beautiful plants flower in fall (autumn) and winter, when a minimum temperature of 50–55°F (10–13°C) should be maintained. In summer they are rested with no watering.

C. persicum has a half-buried "bulb" to 4in (10cm) in diameter, with a dense mass of long-stalked circular leaves marked pale silver; flowers very showy, all hues except yellow-orange, often frilled or double hued; to 12in (30cm).

Eucharis
AMAZON LILY

This tropical lily combines glossy, evergreen paddle-shaped leaves with fragrant daffodil-like flowers of pure white. It prefers filtered light, high humidity, and minimum winter temperature of 60°F (15°C).

E. grandiflora has flowers about 3in (7cm) in diameter, up to six per stalk, height 18in (45cm).

Eucomis
PINEAPPLE LILY

Curious but very ornamental greenish flower-spikes, each topped by a tuft of leafy green bracts like that on a pineapple, give rise to this bulb's common name. The cut flowers are long-lasting. Easily managed, the plants flower in summer from large masses of foliage and die back in fall (autumn). Strong light (sun if possible), a rich compost, and plenti-ful water are their chief requirements. Minimum temperature 35°F (2°C).

E. comosa spikes 2ft (60cm) tall with densely packed, greenish-cream

flowers, often flushed pink. Leaves to 3in (7cm) wide and 18in (45cm) long.

Gloriosa
CLIMBING LILY

Tropical climbing plant from deep-seated bulbs, leaf tips tendril-like. The gaudy scarlet and yellow flowers are like "Turk's cap" liliums, with wavy-edged petals. Easy to grow in

temperatures above 60°F (15°C). Likes a loose rich compost and a wire frame to climb on.

G. superba grows to about 6ft (1.8m). Narrow scarlet petals are yellow at base.

Hippeastrum

Sometimes referred to as 'Amaryllis', these include some of the largest flowered of all bulbs with outward-

ABOVE: One of the loveliest bulbs is the Hippeastrum amaryllis with its trumpet-shaped flowers.

facing, broadly trumpet-shaped flowers up to 8in (20cm) across in shades of white to pink, orange-scarlet or deep red.

The petals are often streaked or feathered with another shade. Planted in winter as large dormant bulbs, they produce their first strap-like leaves in early spring at the same time that the thick flower-stalk appears. This terminates in one to four flowers. Strong light is essential, and the rich bulb compost should be allowed to dry on the surface between waterings. For reliable flowering, buy new bulbs every year. Minimum temperature 45°F (7°C).

H. x hortorum a collective name for the large-flowered hybrids, stems to 2ft 6in (75cm) high.

Lilium

Liliums vary in how they adapt to conservatory culture but some of the most spectacular. large-flowered varieties do well indoors. However, they must be kept cool during the bulbs' dormant period, generally at a temperature of around 40–45°F (4–7°C)—an unheated cellar or even the cold drawer of your refrigerator will do. As soon as shoots appear, bring indoors to a temperature of 60°F (15°C) increasing as the season advances.

Oriental hybrids mostly have a single stem 3–6ft (90cm–1.8m) tall with outward-facing blooms up to 10in (25cm) across, white to gold or crimson.

Polianthes
TUBEROSE

One of the most popular scented flowers, the tuberose is mainly seen nowadays in the form of cut blooms for sale. It makes a rather ungainly plant with a sparse tuft of narrow fleshy leaves, from the middle of which grows a tall, thick hollow flower-spike. Flowering in summer, the plant then produces lateral shoots which flower the following year. It should be grown in a large pot and watered and fed freely while making growth. A sunny position is essential. Minimum temperature 35°F (2°C).

P. tuberosa thick tuberous stem, narrow curled leaves, flower-spike up to 3ft (1m) tall; flowers white, single or double.

Scadoxus
BLOOD FLOWER

Perhaps better known under the name *Haemanthus,* these tropical African bulbs arouse admiration whenever they are flowered successfully. Individual orange to red flowers are small but very profuse, packed into large globe-like or brush-like heads which appear either with or before the new leaves in late spring or summer. Blood flowers need warm conditions, strong light, and rich well-drained compost, watered freely except in winter. Minimum temperature 50°F (10°C).

S. multiflorus (syn. *Haemanthus katherinae*) has a 6–8in (15–20cm) diameter globe of orange to cinnabar-red flowers, on a stalk less than 1ft

(30cm) high, from a rosette of short broad leaves.

Sprekelia
JACOBEAN LILY

This lovely Mexican bulb has deep scarlet flowers, carried singly, and somewhat orchid-like in shape. In a wide pot the plant will multiply and thrive for several years before repotting is necessary. Bulbs are planted in fall (autumn) and overwintered at 45–50°F (7–10°C), so a cool conservatory suits them best.

S. formosissima grows to 15in (40cm), leaves narrow, flower 4in (10cm) across.

Zantedeschia
ARUM LILY

These beautiful flowers grow from short underground rhizomes and have broad, soft, usually arrow-shaped leaves, spotted white in some species. The "flower" is a white, yellow, or pink bract wrapped around a finger-shaped spike on which the tiny true flowers are borne. Small children may suffer painful swelling of lips and throat if they try to eat the flowers. A cool conservatory suits the the plant if winter temperature is 45°F (7°C) or above.

Z. aethiopica (white arum) grows to 3ft (1m) tall, the pure white "flower" to 8in (20cm) long.

Z. elliottiana (yellow arum) is 2ft (60cm) or less, leaves densely white-spotted, "flower" bright yellow.

Z. rehmannii (pink arum) 18in (45cm), less vigorous, "flower" pale pink.

CLIMBERS

Cissus
WATER VINE

Includes several of the most easily grown climbers, valued as quick greenery and for their interesting leaf shapes. Climbing by tendrils, the new shoots can elongate rapidly and need support such as wires; or they can be pinched back frequently to keep the plant shrubby. They prefer warm conditions and reasonable light levels but can tolerate poor light. Minimum temperature 50°F (10°C).

C. antarctica (kangaroo vine) very vigorous with large, oval sharply toothed leaves, shiny above; new shoots with rust-brown hairs.

C. discolor a weak-stemmed vine with beautiful heart-shaped leaves, dark red beneath, dark green overlaid silver above. More tender; minimum temperature 60°F (15°C). Water sparingly.

C. rhombifolia (grape ivy) like *C. antarctica* but more compact, leaves with three leaflets. **'Ellen Danica'** is a form with larger, lobed leaflets.

Clerodendrum
BLEEDING HEART VINE

Most clerodendrums are shrubs but the one usually grown as an indoor plant is a twining vine. Coming from tropical Africa, it requires warmth and humidity but will reward good treatment by a show of strikingly beautiful flower-clusters, each flower consisting of a large pure white calyx from which emerges a small but brilliant scarlet corolla. It is usual to train the plant on stakes or a wire frame but it can also be allowed to twine up wires to ceiling height. Bright light is essential for flower production, and the plant should be watered frequently in summer but sparingly in winter.

C. thomsoniae twining climber to 10ft (3m), glossy heart-shaped leaves to 6in (15cm) long.

Cobaea
CUP-AND-SAUCER VINE

A flowering vine that has a certain subdued beauty, cup-and-saucer vine is so named for the large saucer-like calyx of its bell-shaped flower. Another interesting feature is the change in hue as the blooms age, from pale greenish yellow to dull purple, with several shades generally present at any one time. Available as seed, it is often grown as an annual, making rapid growth in spring and summer, and taking up considerable space. Needs good light. Minimum temperature 45°F (7°C).

C. scandens tendril climber to 10ft (3m), leaves each consisting of four large leaflets and terminating in a branched tendril. Flowers carried singly, 2in (5cm) across.

Ipomoea
MORNING GLORY

Although the plants may be rather rank and weedy in appearance, some of the morning glories have flowers of such a beautiful clear blue and so delicate in structure that they will always be granted indoor space by those who appreciate such fleeting beauty. Opening before dawn, the flowers start to shrivel by early afternoon. Although perennial vines, morning glories are commonly treated as annuals and raised from seed in spring. A sunny position is essential, also plenty of water and fertilizing. Run string or wires to ceiling height for the stems to twine on. Minimum temperature 45°F (7°C).

I. tricolor 'Heavenly Blue' soft-stemmed twining vine to 10ft (3m) or more, leaves heart-shaped. Flowers 3in (7cm) across, pale sky-blue with white in the middle.

Mandevilla
DIPLADENIA

Tropical American climbers with milky sap and large, long-lasting pink flowers, several varieties of these are becoming increasingly popular as indoor plants. Although twining climbers, they can be kept to a very compact size and will produce blooms over a long season. They need warmth and bright light, but will tolerate moderately cool winter temperatures if kept fairly dry. Minimum temperature 50°F (10°C).

M. 'Alice du Pont' hybrid variety, climbing to 7ft (2m), leaves oval, 4in long, strongly wrinkled. Flowers bright rose-pink, 3in (7cm) across, in clusters.

M. sanderi climbs to about 4ft (1.2m) with shiny oval 3in (7cm) leaves.

Flowers 2in (5cm) across, rose-pink with cream throat. A darker magenta-pink variety has recently become available.

Passiflora
PASSIONFLOWER, PASSIONFRUIT

Since first encountered by early European explorers of the Americas, the intricate structure of passionflowers has aroused wonderment. Priests saw them as aids to religious teaching, with the three-branched style representing the Holy Trinity and the ring of bristles Christ's crown of thorns. All vigorous tendril climbers producing masses of foliage, among which the solitary flowers are scattered. Some produce edible fruit but the fruit of most others is inedible or poisonous. They need strong light, plentiful watering, and feeding at regular intervals. A sturdy frame or wire trellis is required for support. Minimum temperature 50°F (10°C).

P. caerulea (blue passionflower) climber to 10ft (3m), long slender shoots with five-lobed shiny leaves, flowers purple-blue and pale green, 3in (7cm) wide.

P. coccinea (scarlet passionflower) climber to 10ft (3m), dense massof dull dark green leaves, scarlet flowers 3in (7cm) wide. Needs winter heat.

P. edulis (passionfruit) is one of several edible species; to 10ft (3m), dense glossy foliage, purple and green flowers, dull purple fruit.

Stephanotis

A tropical twiner with milky sap, stephanotis bears pure white waxy flowers with the most delicious sweet perfume—traditionally used in bridal bouquets, it is grown commercially under

glass for sale as cut flowers. It likes
bright light but preferably not direct
sun, a rich open compost, and sustained
warmth and humidity in spring and
summer together with plentiful watering. Train on a wire frame in a pot or on
wires standing off walls. Minimum
temperature 55°F (13°C).

S. floribunda is the only species,
climbing to 7ft (2m) or more, leaves
leathery, 3in (7cm) long; 1in (2.5cm)
wide flowers in dense clusters.

Syngonium

Also known under the older name
Nephthytis, syngoniums are a group of
tropical climbers, related to philodendrons, which cling by aerial roots. As
indoor plants go they are great sur-
vivors, the tough fleshy stems able to
live for months with little or no water
and inadequate light. More kindly conditions are needed, though, for a good
display of foliage. Although usually
trained up a bark pole or similar support, some varieties can be pinched
back to a compact shape and do not
need to climb. They prefer warmth and
humidity but not excessive watering for
active growth. Minimum temperature
55°F (13°C).

S. podophyllum climber to 6ft (1.8m),
usually seen in juvenile form with broad
arrowhead-shaped leaves, but if allowed
to climb high develops leaves with two
additional smaller leaflets. '**Emerald
Gem**' is more compact with greenish
white zones along leaf veins. '**Frosty**'
has almost white leaves with a narrow
green rim.

ABOVE: A combination of white and gloss green foliage makes the Madagascar chaplet flower
(Stephanotis floribunda) *ideal for display.*

OPPOSITE: A wonderful creeper that is as edible as it is attractive — Passiflora edulis.

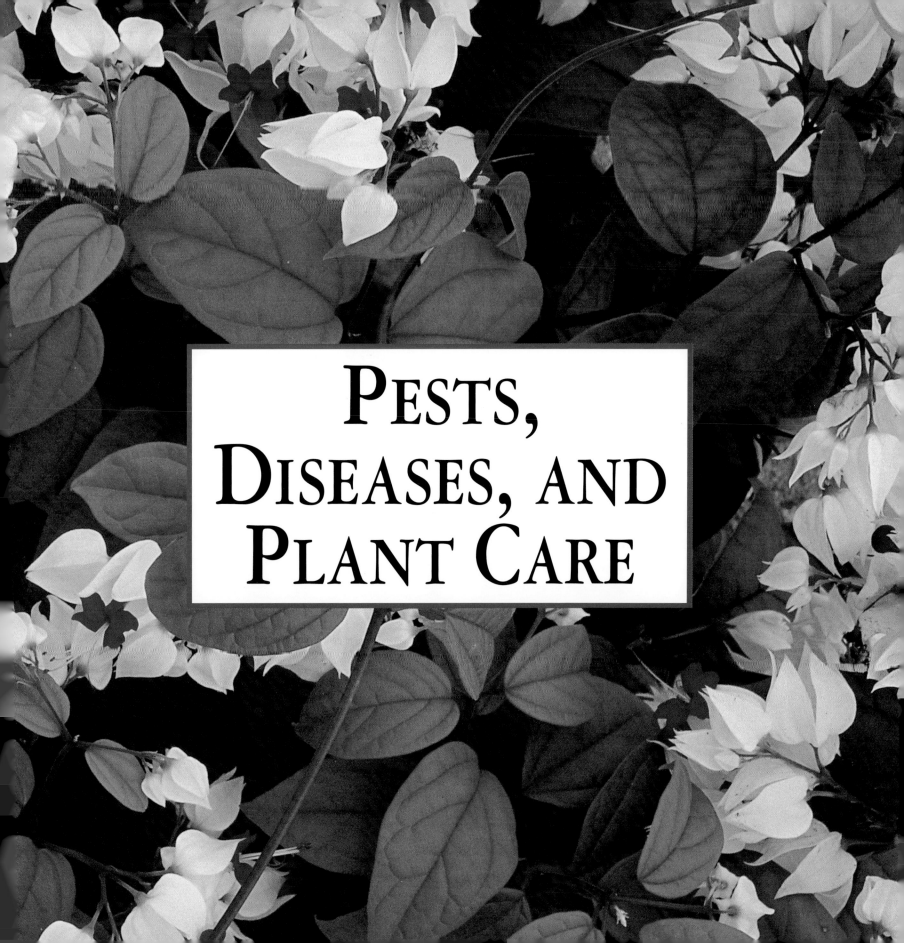

PESTS, DISEASES, AND PLANT CARE

Prevention and cures

Plants are like human beings—they need tender loving care. Give plants light, sunshine, nourishment, water, and encouragement and they will thrive. Once you have planned and planted your conservatory, it is important to draw up a routine of care and maintenance to ensure that your plants thrive.

Conservatory plants exist in an enclosed, hot and dry environment and it is in these conditions that pests and diseases spread easily from an unhealthy plant to a healthy one. As a precaution, make sure you thoroughly cleanse any containers and pots that have been used before. This will help rid your plants of obstinate diseases living in old soil. The sight of unhealthy plants is enough to discourage even the keenest and most patient gardener, so quick action is strongly recommended.

OPPOSITE: Exotic palms such as this Strelitzia nicolai *need warmth and sunlight but is wise to watch the amount of direct sunlight as the edges of the leaves may turn brown as they have here.*
PREVIOUS PAGE: Both the leaf shape and delicate flower shape are immensely appealing in this fine example of bleeding heart vine (Clerodendrum thomsoniae).

The best prevention is to make sure that you buy the healthiest, strongest specimens from your local plant nursery. Do not buy a plant that has the slightest tinge of yellow on a leaf, or looks wilted. Find out as much as you can about the plant's preferences for light, shade, heat, or cool conditions, and place the plant where it will grow happily. You will notice after a short time if the plant is thriving where you placed it and whether or not you are giving it too much or too little water. With automatic watering systems and electronically operated shade systems, caring for your investment can become a pleasant part of your daily routine.

Signs that will tell you the plant is unhealthy:

1. A wilting or dropping leaf or bloom is a sure sign that something is wrong. Act immediately. Water the plant and spray all the leaves, especially if you have not been diligent about watering regularly.
2. Yellowing leaves are a sign that the plant is in a draft. Plants hate drafts, as do people. Yellowing may also mean overwatering. Feed with a plant nutrient.
3. If the soil is shrinking away from the outer rim of the pot or container, immerse the pot completely in a sink full of water—not too cold, not warm. Room temperature is best.
4. Look at the roots. Are they rotting because you have overwatered? It does happen. Are there insects in the soil? If you have been overfeeding the plant, salts build up in the soil. The best remedy is to re-pot the plant, place in a different position in the conservatory, and watch its progress.

PLANT PESTS

Pest invasion in a conservatory can be disastrous. Generally, careful and regular spraying keeps the individual plants healthy. Look for organic rather than chemical products, but if you have to resort to chemicals, use them when you are not about to use the conservatory to entertain.

Ants: Invaders from outdoors, ants do no harm to plants but are capable of spreading aphids from one plant to another. Check the plant roots to see if any ants have bored in. Use ant bait to kill them.

Aphids: Tiny green, yellow, or black insects. One of the most common plant pests, aphids like tender new growth. They suck the plant's sap which inhibits growth and turns the leaves

ABOVE: In a steamy environment, bugs spread easily from one plant to another so it is wise to examine precious plants on the top and the underneath of leaves for signs of unwelcome small creatures.

yellow. The best way to treat this problem is to wash the plant's leaves thoroughly with soapy water. Use a mild detergent and follow with a clear rinse. You may prefer to use a dimethoate solution.

Caterpillars: Leaf-eating larvae which are highly destructive to plants. Remove caterpillaes by hand, or dust with carbaryl.

Cyclamen mites: Common pests, difficult to spot. Stunted and/or distorted leaves and flowers give you a clue. Difficult to control safely. If plants are affected, destroy them.

Earwigs: Holes that appear overnight in petals and leaves mean earwigs are present. Dust flower blooms. Using ant bait is recommended, placing it near to the cracks and holes where the earwigs live.

Root mealy bugs: Small, oval-shaped insects that attack a plant's roots. Check the roots for white patches or specks of "wool" when re-potting. Drench your potting mixture with pesticide if there is even a hint of these bugs.

Scale insects: Sap-eating, these are found on the underside of leaves. Rub the insects out by hand, using a soapy rag. It takes patience, but is reassuring.

Sciarid-fly maggots: Small, black-headed worms sometimes called fungus gnats, these like to eat plant roots. Damp humid conditions cause an

ABOVE: Make it a habit to regularly search through the leaves to spot insects and mealy bugs before they move in permanently.

outbreak. Check the potting mixture for eggs and treat it with a recommended mixture. Ask your local garden supplier for the latest effective product.

Slugs and snails: Leaf-eaters that attack seedlings. Use slug or snail bait to destroy them.

Spider mites: Miniscule mites whose effects are quickly identified when you find yellow mottled leaves which will inevitably brown and shrivel. A fine white web covers the underside of plant leaves. Hot and dry conditions encourage these creatures. Cut off badly affected leaves and stems. Use an insecticide to treat the rest of the plant.

Thrips: Almost invisible insects that appear as specks producing white

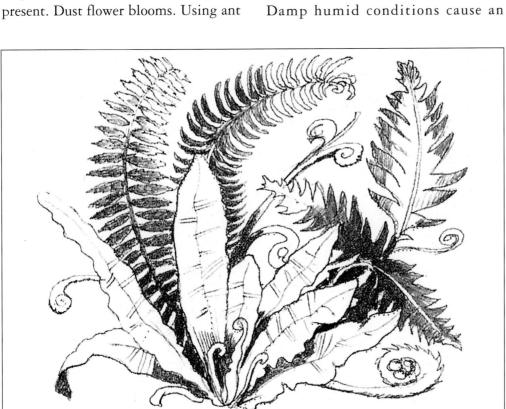

ABOVE: Fern fronds can be damaged by mealy bugs and other pests.

patches surrounded by small black spots on leaves. Treat with insecticide or derris spray.

Weevils: Curved white grubs that feed on plant roots, causing the roots to die. Adults resemble a beetle with a long proboscis or snout. Destroy an infested plant.

White flies: Small, white, waxy flies. The larvae are sap-sucking and produce honeydew, turning leaves yellow. Treat with pyrethrum spray.

PLANT DISEASES

Most of the plant diseases that attack conservatory plants are fungal types, induced by excess moisture and cold. Plants can also be affected by viral diseases spread by insects. These cause stunted growth and leaf distortion. Viral diseases are lethal so afflicted plants must be destroyed quickly. The most common plant diseases and their treatment are as follows:

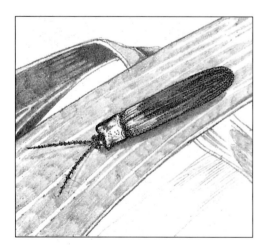

ABOVE: These beetles cause havoc on palm leaves as they chew the leaf tissue in thin lines parallel to the middle rib.

Botrytis: A fungus with the official name of Botrytis cinerea. Has a fluffy, silvery appearance. Disturbing an affected plant causes clouds of spores to rise from it. Remove fungal areas and apply a fungicide.

Leaf spot: Covers foliage with blister-like brown, yellow, or white spots of different sizes resulting from fungi or bacteria. Remove affected leaves and spray with fungicide.

Mildew: Easily identified as white, powder-like mold on leaves, stems, and flowers. Take special care of soft-leaved plants, fruit trees, and bushes. Be careful not to overwater. Certain brands of fungicides are good for controlling mildew. Check the labels and ask the specialist at your local plant store.

Rust: Red-brown spots (on many plants) tell you that rust is present. Treat with a dithane spray as soon as you spot rust.

Sooty mold: Sap-sucking insects such as aphid and scale are forerunners to sooty mold. Try fungicidal sprays to kill it, but if the unsightly mold remains remove it using a cloth soaked in soapy water or a fungicide solution.

ORGANIC ALTERNATIVES

In these days of chemical sprays and formulas, it is easy to find a quick-fix solution to any garden ailment. However, the thoughtful gardener always looks for an organic alternative to drowning the plants in chemical mixes. Manufacturers have responded to this desire for natural gardening, and new products including non-

harmful insecticides and fungicides are constantly appearing on the shelves at gardening stores.

It is as well to remember that every planting scheme in a conservatory is a small ecosystem, with a fine balance between the healthy growth of plants and disease or pest infestation. Insects themselves have a way of working to balance this ecosystem; one type preys on another and this keeps the numbers under control. When we spray against one insect, we invariably also kill others in the chain, destroying the fine, natural balance.

There are several positive steps you can take to enhance the natural process:

• Change your attitude. Do not expect perfection in the conservatory. Accept that a certain percentage of the crop may be damaged slightly or eaten by predators.

• Prior to planting, always prepare the soil or potting mixture well, and keep a good supply of organic matter to build up and feed the mixture.

• Choose only healthy specimens when potting because weakened plants are susceptible to damage and disease.

• Check plants regularly for signs of disease or insect infestation. Do not wait until it is too late.

• Maintain the plants with routine watering and feeding.

• Keep the area around plants free from weeds. Clean cultivation is vital in the chain of pest prevention.

• Consider using organic fly traps, baits, and sprays.

• Keep weed growth clear from the base of plants affected by fungal disease. Good air circulation helps greatly to prevent this.

ORGANIC TIPS

• Manually remove aphids, or spray with a soapy solution through a suitable nozzle.

• Use shallow saucers of flat beer to attract and kill snails and slugs.

• Put fine line of sawdust or holly leaves around groups of pots to deter snails and slugs.

• Boil rhubarb leaves in water, then dilute the mixture and spray it onto plants to discourage aphids and caterpillars.

• Make sprays from soap, washing soda, or nicotine.

• Pyrethrum-based sprays are effective against a wide range of leaf-chewing insects. These sprays are environmentally friendly.

• White oil is a harmless spray against scale.

• Sulphur and copper sprays are also safe to use against fungal diseases.

THE IMPORTANCE OF LIGHT

Plants require light to carry out photosynthesis which causes growth in plants. Each plant's natural requirements varies: cacti will soak up sunshine while plants that grow in the shade on the floor of tropical rainforests get just glimpses of daylight. Read about the conditions each plant prefers and re-create these conditions in your conservatory. Keep shade-loving plants

ABOVE: Potted plants need regular inspections for scales and mealy bugs. Take them into the bright light, look under and on top of leaves, feeling the stem and leaf surfaces for lumps which may be the invading scales. Mealy bugs and red spider mites are attracted to the weeping fig (Ficus benjamina). Remove badly affected leaves and wash the plant with a soapy solution.

out of direct sunlight, and in a cooler area. You will notice that its leaves drop if there is too much light.

On the other hand, if your plant becomes weak and its blooms are pale in appearance it is obviously not getting the sun it requires. Try it in a sunny position and note the difference.

Because of its glass structure, the conservatory floods with light during the day and the amount must be carefully regulated. Shade blinds are essential if your conservatory is located in full sun all day. There are many types of blinds available, so check with your conservatory supplier for the correct advice for your situation. There are also certain brands of paint which, when used on the interior of glass panels, can help to keep sunlight out. Use green rather than white as it is more effective as a blockout.

Shade can also be created by cleverly planting small trees and shrubs with lots of foliage along the side where light floods in. Check the growing conditions of these. Make sure they will survive lots of sun and you will have created a splendid environment naturally. Remember, too, that sunlight is less intense in the middle of the conservatory, away from the windows and arrange your plants accordingly. Depending upon the height and angle of the roof, you may need to reduce the amount of light coming through with some kind of shade provider. This may reduce light intensity (but not necessarily the temperature) by half and more in the middle of

the conservatory. Of course, this figure varies depending upon whether you have a south or north-facing conservatory; east or west-facing structures get strong sunshine only in the early morning and late afternoon. What you must think carefully about when placing plants is that the sun will be brighter in the summer than it is in winter.

The leaves and flowers of a plant search for the light source, so to make sure the plant grows evenly turn the plant in a clockwise direction (say, 30 degrees) on a regular basis.

TROPICAL AND SUBTROPICAL PLANTS

You may choose to grow exotic plants that need more than the natural light source, especially during winter. In that case, a booster light source will be necessary. Some gardeners recommend using artificial light to grow tropical plants year-round. If you decide to do that, make sure you feed the plants appropriately. However, it is not a good idea to treat cacti in this way, since they need a quiet growth time. Study growth information on cacti so that you will recognize when the plant is in this phase.

WHICH ARTIFICIAL LIGHT TO USE?

Heated light bulbs or fluorescent tubes are best to supplement natural light, especially in winter in cooler climates. Turn on the lights for four to six hours a night for foliage plants; six to eight hours for flowering types. Straight

tubes, flat panels, and rings have been designed for use over plants growing in bowls or tubs. Look for tubes recommended for use with plants. These give out light in red and blue wavelengths which plants prefer. Some have an electric timer switch which is great for pre-setting and controlling the amount of heat and light.

Check the wattage of any light you decide upon. As a general rule, place two tubes about 6 inches (15cm) apart for each regular-size plant.

Ask your local lighting specialists if they stock intensified fluorescent tubes (very-high-output, VHO) tubes as these are recommended for use with plants that enjoy plenty of heat.

Unobtrusive fluorescent tubes attached under shelves can be helpful to the growth of special plants. It is often effective to highlight plants grouped under shelves, and this can look wonderful at night. Buy special heat-giving screw-in fittings for conventional lights or use contemporary spotlights (depending upon the style of your conservatory), and suspend them at a reasonable distance above the plants. You may need to adjust the distance, but careful observation will allow you to judge how well the plant is faring.

MOISTURE IN THE AIR

The higher the temperature in the conservatory, the higher the level of humidity required. For ferns in cool conservatories, and for tropical species in particular, a high humidity level is essential. Air humidity is measured on a scale from 0 to 100—0 percent being dry and 100 percent being full saturation level. Plants usually require a humidity level of 50–60 percent. Succulents require 35–40 percent. You may like to invest in a hygrometer, which shows the level of humidity on a dial.

Serious gardeners who have plant-only conservatories check the humidity levels frequently, and are sometimes seen splashing the floor with water to increase humidity. Where this is not practicable, spray blooms and leaves regularly with a mist spray.

FEEDING THE PLANT

As long as you were careful when choosing the compost or soil in which to pot your plant at the beginning of its life in the conservatory, the plant will not need to be fed continually. Plants need an adequate supply of minerals to grow successfully, and it is this mineral content that you must keep an eye on as the plant grows in the restricted conditions of a pot or container. A good-quality soil-based potting mixture is preferable as it contains the three elements necessary for growth—potash, phosphates, and nitrates (particularly essential for leafy plants because they promote new leaf shoots).

There are plenty of good brands of prepared fertilizers on the market, so read the package label before buying to make sure that the mixture has the correct elements your particular plant needs.

When to feed is a matter of observation. There is a general rule, though, for the majority of plants: feed the plant with the recommended mixture just before it is about to burst into leaf and flowers. A good feed every two weeks during this period will produce excellent results. However, be careful not to overfeed as you could end up with too much leaf growth and few flowers.

FERTILIZERS

Organic fertilizers generally consist of a smelly mixture of well-aged manure, dried blood, bone meal, and fish meal. The good news is that you can buy these mixtures ready-to-use from your garden supplier, or you can use your home-made garden compost.

Dried blood, as gruesome as it sounds, is the best organic fertilizer. Bone and fish meal contain phosphate combined with nitrogen and potash.

Chemical mixtures are sold in liquid, powder, and pellet forms.

It is a matter of personal preference as to which you use. Chemical fertilizers act quickly, but the slower response organic mixtures are effective for a longer period.

Compound fertilizers combine natural and synthetic elements to create an excellent food.

Check the packaging instructions when using these mixtures. Apply fertilizers close to the roots of the plant, and be careful not to touch the leaves as you could damage them.

To ensure a good level of humidity for individual plants, there is a choice of methods.
1. Bury the pot in damp potting mixture. 2. Place pot on trays of wet gravel.
3. Stand pot in a bowl of water, ensuring the pot is raised just above the water line.

Index

Photography Credits

The Garden Picture Library (Clive Boursnell) front cover
The Garden Picture Library (Ron Sutherland/designer: Duane Paul Design Team) back cover
The Garden Picture Library (Steven Wooster) pp.2-3
Phillip H. Ennis Photography p.4
Derek Fell p.5
The Garden Picture Library (Mayer/Le Scanff) p.7
Arcaid (Lucinda Lambton) p.9
The Garden Picture Library (John Miller) p.14
Elizabeth Whiting and Associates p.16
The Garden Picture Library (John Miller) p.18
The Garden Picture Library (Clive Boursnell) p.19
The Garden Picture Library (John Miller) p.20
Boys Syndication pp. 22-23
The Garden Picture Library (Steven Wooster) p 24
Boys Syndication p.27
Boys Syndication pp.32-33
Elizabeth Whiting and Associates p.34
The Garden Picture Library (John Miller) p.38
The Garden Picture Library (Brian Carter) p.40
The Garden Picture Library (John Miller) p.44
Boys Syndication p.48
Elizabeth Whiting and Associates p.52
The Garden Picture Library (Steven Wooster) p.53
Eric Crichton p.54
The Garden Picture Library (John Miller) p.60
The Garden Picture Library (Zara McCalmont) p.64
The Garden Picture Library (Ron Sutherland) p. 65
Harry Smith Horticultural Photographic Collection p.66
Lansdowne Publishing (Andrew Payne/stylist: Anne-Maree Unwin) pp.70-71 and p.72; p.74, p.78
Ivy Hansen Photography pp.76-77, p.80, p.81, p.82, p.83, p.84, p.86, p.87, p.89, p.90, p.92, p.93, p.94, p.96, p.97, p.99, p.100, p.103, p.104, p.105, p.106, p.107, p.108, p.109, p.112, p.113, pp.114-115, pp.116-117, p.121
Andrew Lawson p.118
Edifice endpapers

The publishers extend their thanks to the following companies for providing pictorial material:
Oak Leaf Conservatories, England: pp.10-11 (John Miller), p.56
Vale Conservatories, England: pp. 12, 31, 39, 15 (illustrations)

First published in the United Kingdom in 1993 by
ANAYA Publishers Ltd
3rd Floor, Strode House
44-50 Osnaburgh Street
London NW1 3ND

Originally published by Lansdowne Publishing Pty Ltd

Designer: Kathie Baxter Smith
Illustrators: Valerie Price,
Sue Ninham and Mike Gorman

British Library Cataloguing-in-Publication Data:

Bryan, Lynn
Conservatory Gardening:
Complete Practical Guide
I. Title
635

ISBN 1-85470-185-1

Designed on Quark Xpress in Garamond 3

Printed in Singapore by Kyodo Printing Co. (S'pore) Pte Ltd

Front cover: This traditional conservatory features glossy green leaves and ivy trailing from a beautiful rectangular free-standing planter.
Back cover: An oasis of calm in palms.
Endpapers: Trellis placed against a cream painted wall is the perfect vehicle for a climber such as the gorgeous passionflower.
Title page: Elegant wicker furniture sits amongst a mass of fuchsias, maidenhair ferns and geraniums.
Page 4: A golden birdcage is the focus of attention, surrounded by hydrangeas in full bloom. The white window frames are in the reproduction Gothic style.
Page 5: Clay pots contain a display of bright and cheerful mixed gloxinia plants.

Acknowledgments

To Leo, for the laughter

Thanks are due to Tony Rodd, plant expert, without whom the plant lists would not have been so cleverly chosen. And to John Patrick, author and landscape designer, who designed the planting schemes; to The Country Trader, Paddington, to Jenkins Distributors, Bonds Nursery, Cotswold Garden Furniture, and Sheridan Furnishing Fabrics, NSW. Thanks also to Jane Tresidder for being an inspiration.